La Conquistadora

La Conquistadora

Unveiling the History
of Santa Fe's
Six Hundred Year Old
Religious Icon

Jaima Chevalier

SANTA FE

Sunstone books may be purchased for educational, business, or sales promotional use.
For information please write: Special Markets Department, Sunstone Press,
P.O. Box 2321, Santa Fe, New Mexico 87504-2321.

Book and Cover design ◊ Vicki Ahl
Body typeface ◊ Constantia ◊ ◊ Display typeface ◊ Melbourne Serial
Printed on acid free paper

Library of Congress Cataloging-in-Publication Data

Chevalier, Jaima, 1958-
   La conquistadora : unveiling the history of Santa Fe's six hundred year old religious icon / by Jaima
Chevalier.
      p. cm.
   Includes bibliographical references.
   ISBN 978-0-86534-789-2 (softcover : alk. paper)
   1. Conquistadora. 2. Mary, Blessed Virgin, Saint--Art. 3. Mary, Blessed Virgin, Saint--Devotion
to--New Mexico--Santa Fe. 4. Cathedral of San Francisco de Asis (Santa Fe, N.M.)--History.
5. Catholic Church--New Mexico--Santa Fe--History. 6. Santa Fe (N.M.)--Church history. I. Title.
   BT660.S45C53 2010
   247--dc22

                        2010040585

Published in

WWW.SUNSTONEPRESS.COM
SUNSTONE PRESS / POST OFFICE BOX 2321 / SANTA FE, NM 87504-2321 /USA
(505) 988-4418 / ORDERS ONLY (800) 243-5644 / FAX (505) 988-1025

Dedication

For Clara Garcia and for Frances,
along with her little brother,
the "real" Chevalier,
for helping me to understand how
La Conquistadora belongs to all of us.

Events far-reaching enough to people all space, whose end is nonetheless tolled when one man dies, may cause us wonder. But something, or an infinite number of things, dies in every death, unless the universe is possessed of a memory, as the theosophists have supposed.

—Jorge Luis Borges, "The Witness," *Dream Tigers*

Contents

Foreword

La Conquistadora is a sculpted wooden image of the Virgin Mary. As the nation's oldest Marian statue, she is an enduring icon of Santa Fe's famed fusion of art, history, and spiritualism. She was brought by ox cart to Santa Fe in 1626 after a six-month journey from Mexico, but her many adventures trace her provenance back even further. As the central figure in Santa Fe's annual Fiesta, the celebration in her honor is supposed to have been the fulfillment of a promise made by don Diego de Vargas after he sought her intercession for a peaceful reconquest of the city after the Pueblo Revolt of 1680. However, modernly, her role encompasses many attributes and reaches into many corners of New Mexico history, crossing dimensions of time and space in the same way that her gaze is said to penetrate the soul.

La Conquistadora is cared for by *La Cofradía de la Conquistadora*, a confraternity of men and women who safeguard the image and provide for its preservation and maintenance. A so-called "secret society," the group's historic antecedents date back many centuries, but in New Mexico, the group's history of veneration surrounding La Conquistadora begins to appear in records in the 1650s, with the dramatic story of her rescue and exile during the Pueblo Revolt of 1680 underscoring the confraternity's age-old allegiance to their patroness.

The confraternity is led by a *mayordomo* who organizes processions, acts as caretaker for La Conquistadora's chapel, and provides for her upkeep. The group also elects a *sacristana* to act of custodian of the garments, crowns, and belongings of the statue. The sacristana, who is also responsible for changing the statue's attire according to the liturgical calendar, oversees a rapidly growing wardrobe of clothing made for the statue by the many devoted followers who attribute some form of miracle to her divine intercession.

Preface

During the 1970s, I studied Latin at Santa Fe High School for four years with Pedro Ribera-Ortega. Learning a long-dead language served no career goal or specific purpose in my curriculum, but Ribera-Ortega's custom of producing an annual Roman banquet at the school, where all the students wore togas and swilled grape juice out of jugs, appealed to my sense of drama, history, and symbolism, so I enrolled in his Latin classes.

When "Mr. Ortega" gave us our lessons (to this day, I can recite the pledge of allegiance in Latin), he would often seem sorely beset by the cares of the world and burdened by off-campus concerns. Later, I learned that he had extremely important duties at St. Francis Cathedral (now a Basilica), none of which I understood, but which kept him extremely busy year-round. I discovered that Mr. Ortega had a much more exalted and mysterious title because he was serving, as he had for many years, as *mayordomo*, leader of the ancient *La Cofradía de la Conquistadora*, an organization that is devoted to the care and preservation of La Conquistadora, the nation's oldest Marian statue, preserved in the La Conquistadora Chapel at Santa Fe's St. Francis of Assisi Cathedral Basilica.

Of Our Lady, shadowy images came to my mind: processions witnessed, as if in a dream, of her standard-bearers during Fiesta processions and other solemn occasions. But, what, truly, did I know of her? The romance of the Christian knighthood that protected her was far more intriguing than the pageantry of high school toga parties.

Pedro Ribera-Ortega receiving the *"El Adelantado"* award from the New Mexico Hispanic Culture Preservation League in April of 2001. Photograph by Dolores Valdez de Pong.

I determined to learn more and to compile facts about her origins, the stories of her existence, and the people who serve her. What I learned along the way is vastly different from what I set out to do. I began by compiling new evidence about La Conquistadora that had come to light since publication of the definitive work on this subject: *Our Lady of the Conquest*, written in 1948 by Fray Angélico Chávez (reissued in 2010 by Sunstone Press), and his companion volume from 1954, the quasi-autobiographical *La Conquistadora: The Autobiography of an Ancient Statue* (revised and reissued in 1983 by Sunstone Press).

The importance of La Conquistadora is as compelling today as it was then: this powerful symbol, the nation's oldest Madonna, deserves special study due to her proximity to the history of two continents and of the nation's oldest capital. She witnessed, as it were, more than three centuries of the tumultuous past that created the social upheaval and clash of cultures that has now been transmuted into a place known as being in the vanguard of social reconciliation and justice, Santa Fe, New Mexico.

I originally wanted merely to update Chávez's work with new empirical evidence about La Conquistadora. I believed that the material deserved a certain scientific detachment, and that undertaking a strictly objective analysis of recent developments; such as the scientific analysis of the wood used to make her, the x-ray examination of her interior structure, and the 1973 kidnapping, would amplify understanding of La Conquistadora's hold on the public's imagination and illuminate her legend.

But as I endeavored to catalogue the memories of things that happened to her, around her, and about her, I was not prepared for the inner journey this quest triggered in me. I could not separate the strong feelings I experienced from the material, so I beg the reader's indulgence for places where emotion about the material colored the text, resist it as I might.

The objective facts of her existence have transcended mere history, earthly confines, and science to achieve something more: proof, if you will, of the spiritual lore that has made her a legend; that she is not only an actual statue but simultaneously a symbol, a prayer and a proof of abiding love to many. She is not a mere *bulto*, a long-dead block of wood, but a living symbol of faith, visited sometimes by over 100 people per hour.

The subject matter of this book made me a student of geography, as I shuttled back and forth along the dizzying trails of La Conquistadora's many journeys across two continents in two hemispheres. Any student of La Conquistadora must be a time traveler of sorts, seeking an understanding of how her travels over as many as six different centuries have contributed to her mythology.

But most of all, Our Lady brings its subjects on a spiritual journey with her, exploring pathways to the human heart, learning that some things cross all dimensions of time and space, and drift into that ethereal continuum, that drift called the infinite, which divides mere mortals from immortality but which unites us with eternity.

Acknowledgments

Lea Ann Boone

La Cofradía de la Conquistadora and its officers

Ignacio Garcia, Mayordomo of La Cofradía

Terry García, Sacristana

Robin Farwell Gavin

Peggy Humpheys

Consuelo Hernández

Carrie Lynn Korzak

Rev. Monsignor Jerome Martínez y Alire

Marina Ochoa

Dolores Valdez de Pong

Inez Russell

Arnold Vigil

Andrea "Drew" Bacigalupa

and to

Pedro Ribera-Ortega, *in memoriam*

Libros, ¡ay! sin los cuales

No podemos vivir: sed siempre, siempre,

Los tácitos amigos de mis días.

(Books, Oh! Without which

We cannot live; be always, always,

The silent friends of all my days.)

—Amado Nervo

Prologue

Doña Josefa López Sambrano de Grijalva drew the ties of her cloak to a point, closing the cowl over her face like a monk. A strange smoke curled beneath her nostrils as the wind rattled across *La Parróquia's* rafters. As she drew in her breath to hold it, the roof beams seemed to shift, drawing a bolt of moonlight down into the dark chapel. Her hands trembled as she reached into the *nicho*, drawing the heavy wood figure from its sanctuary in the wall. How best to hide her? Slinging the statue over her back seemed wrong. Should she cradle her like a small child? She took a shawl from her bag and wrapped the figure as best she could, while the darkening sky drew a veil of shadow over the statue's face.

Moonlight glinted off the adobe bricks as she slipped outside, but in the shadows near the buildings, Josefa could feel Our Lady's eyes upon her every movement. Josefa crept along buildings until she reached the *Casas Reales del Palacio* and gave no sound as she slipped into the fortified compound. Padre had told her to place Our Lady in the *torreón* where a small makeshift chapel was set up, but when she reached the door, she felt her chest tighten and her heart rise into her throat. Suddenly, she knew it was better to keep Our Lady with her at all times.

Famine stalked the settlers of Villa de Santa Fe as a ten-year drought had parched the land. The long years of privation had given way to frantic activity over the last few days. Po'pay's messengers had been captured and brought to the compound. One bore a strange knotted cord on his person, and a great debate erupted among the settlers. What was the meaning of the cord? Was each knot to represent a day left until the attack was made? Or did each knot count as a certain Pueblo's vote to participate?

Governor Otermín was beset by indecision as the siege wore on. Then word came of tragedy in Taos, at Isleta, and beyond. Devastation and war were at hand, with four hundred settlers and clerics killed in the outlying areas. Some of the scouts that had been sent to warn villagers did not return. The gurgling *acequia* that carried water to the compound had been cut off. Of the thousand people remaining, only one hundred fifty were capable of military service, and attacks continued unabated.

They saddled the horses the next morning. The panic-stricken faces of those straggling into the compound told them all they needed to know: casualties were too great and escape was now the only option. They would ride southward to safety, escaping the Pueblo Revolt, looking back at *El Reyno de la Nueba México*, watching the flames at the *casas reales*, hearing the distant cries, escaping the clashing ring of metal on metal, the muffled groan of man and beast.

Josefa steeled herself for the journey; she alone would carry Our Lady close, as heavy as she was, over hundreds of miles south to safety. The retreat would take them to Isleta, San Lorenzo, San Pedro de Alcántara, and Santísimo Sacramento, El Paso del Norte, and to the mission at Guadalupe del Paso. The journey would be dangerous and fraught with peril, but *deo volente*, Our Lady would be safe, even if her earthly home should burn to the ground.

1

Black and White Magic
and the Chessmen of Spain

Yesterday the abolition of fairies and giants;

The fortress like a motionless eagle eyeing the valley,

The chapel built in the forest;

Yesterday the carving of angels and of frightening gargoyles.

—W.H. Auden, "Spain 1937"

The cause why the Spanishe have destroyed such an infinitie of soules,

hath been onely, that they have helde it for their last scope

and marke to gette golde.

—Bartolomé de las Casas, Dominican Priest

In the conquest of the New World, no one reason can be ascribed to the missions undertaken, the causes that people died for, or the meaning given to these things today. Certainly there was a competition of ideas about the waves of journeys from Columbus onward, and the simplistic litany of "glory, God, and gold" given as the reason for the Spanish intrusion into the New World does not begin to describe the entire spectrum of reasons why worlds began to collide in the fifteenth century when Columbus's ship the *Santa María* ran aground at Caracol Bay in the Caribbean on December 25, 1492.

Other events were converging to set the stage for an epic drama. The marriage of Ferdinand of Aragon and Isabella of Castile had created a political union, while the capture of Granada, the sole remaining Muslim kingdom on Spanish soil, and the expulsion of all unconverted Jews in 1492 had created a religious union that was all-encompassing. For the positive dynamic of Catholicism to prevail; however, the scale would have to tip toward Rome. Instead, the effect of the dispersal of Jewish poets and scholars began to reach into Eastern Europe, Palestine, and even remote parts of New Mexico. An earlier diffusion of Jews helped to develop the Eastern Renaissance in the beginning of the Middle Ages, predating the Italian Renaissance by several centuries. Into each country where the exiled Jewish scholars came, literary historians have found an astounding body of work, as the expatriates learned and wrote in many languages: Hebrew, Aramaic, Greek, Spanish, French, and more. Imperial aggression had inadvertently created a flowering of human expression, and, most importantly for our tale, it created a body and tradition of self-examination and introspection that allow us to understand La Conquistadora's story from many different perspectives.

The Spanish crown's directive to its explorers was a contractual obligation, and established exchanges of land and title to be granted to the man who risked his fortune on the speculation that riches could be had in remote lands. Reports to the crown were colored by optimism and hyperbole: grand stories of streets paved with gold and gentle natives. Columbus wrote of the assistance he received when the ship ran aground: "[they are] so full of love and without greed, and suitable for every purpose, that I assure your Highnesses that I believe that there is no better land in the world, and they are always smiling."

These new souls had to be converted for the glory of the Spanish crown, so men of faith began to populate every expedition. Men of faith are men of letters, so the *conquistador* was not free to venture forth unfettered by spiritual oversight or intellectual reflection. The mercenary aspects of each expedition had to compete with ideas unconnected to material wealth, and, most importantly, these embedded journalists created a vast record of the journeys, often telling a tale that contrasted with the official version of events. In large part because the military and spiritual aspects of each expedition fought for supremacy, the Spanish custom of contemplating and debating the status of the new-found peoples led to the creation of laws dealing with populations in countries yet to be. In *Laws of the Indies* (Law 2, title 1, book 6) promulgated on October 19, 1514, the so-called Indo-Hispano was determined to be a "legitimate race."

In Spain's checkerboard existence, with massive incursions of many peoples over many centuries, swallowing and absorbing a kingdom that expanded and contracted, slowly replacing the crescent moon with the cross, remnants of those deposed from power created a situation where subversive or underground ideas survived, sometimes infiltrating popular discourse. The notion that the Indo-Hispano could be converted and claimed to the Catholic faith, instead of being exterminated, allowed for the possibility of insurrection, treason, and rebellion. In New Mexico, an extraordinary circumstance created a convergence of two groups at odds with their oppressors or captors: the native people and the Sephardic Jews (and to a lesser extent, the *conversos*), all of whom acted as unbiased eyewitnesses to the Spanish incursion. Even if they practiced Catholic customs and rituals, their upbringing and native faith may not have been fully erased, making their understanding of the outside world a reflection of their inner beliefs.

For the dispersed or the dispossessed alike, a history of suffering for their faith gave them an innate ability to question the pious labels covering the expedition, and so we find traces of other faiths in the Catholic story in New Mexico. But the story of La Conquistadora has elements of history, of symbolism, and of human endurance amid suffering and change that give it an almost universal appeal.

From earliest times, in a light cast by fire, the "first face" of the mother of man has been fashioned into likenesses of the archetypal female. As Christianity has spread over the world, the likeness of the Mother of Jesus has likewise been fashioned into many cultures and versions. *La última madre* sometimes reflects the visage of the artist's mother, or a common face of the community, or an idealized beauty of the time. During the great wave of Spanish explorations, nautical iterations of the Virgin and the saints joined their land-faring counterparts and fanned out over the globe, traveling to *las Indias* or *las Américas*, sent on missions by both religious leaders and heads of state. In beginning to study La Conquistadora, this is one of her greatest mysteries: how did she come to be and for what purpose?

The first area to explore is her physical world; the question of what she consists of and how she was manufactured. Additional topics of inquiry include how she inhabits the physical realm, and what spatial relationships comprise her earthly home. Subsequent chapters will turn to her purpose and meaning, since the purpose for which her maker designed her for may have changed over the centuries, as surely as her ownership has changed hands. While originally she was in the care of one custodian, now an elite cadre of caregivers has grown up around her into a select and quasi-secret organization with parallels to other organizations with similar goals but vastly divergent purposes. The purposes that have been ascribed to her have changed as well, and what she was meant to be may be at odds with what she has become.

The official story of her existence and the meaning ascribed to her by church officials and by her proponents hold one place in the La Conquistadora legend. An entire mythology has grown up around her, so much so that her existence is veiled by the shadows of those who protect her from scrutiny and harm. But La Conquistadora cannot be defined solely by the owners or stakeholders in her continued existence, for she has transcended any status as mere chattel to become the belonging of all. She has become an enduring symbol, with value and meaning beyond all original confines. She is not a frozen marionette miming her basic function as the corporeal body of the Blessed Mother, but a fully-realized person who, with her articulated arms, is exalted in popular imagination as a ruler.

La Conquistadora in full regalia, 2009. Photograph by LeRoy N. Sanchez.

Whether envisioned as an angel above, or as the Madonna among us, the Virgin Mary has been perceived as both a reflection of certain values and as the holder of many powers. Although her proponents have conceded the point that manifestations of black and white magic are the oldest and most widespread liturgies among all peoples throughout the world, her champions preach that only the Virgin Mary has been able to coalesce with the divine. In her stationary throne in church, intercessory powers ascribed to her have made her a powerful object of human prayer. But unlike most totems or icons of historic peoples or religions, this saint has the rare power and ability to move among us. For example, during the Crusades, men took her likeness with them into battle, and the rally for lost souls sounded from the pole where she was held aloft. So because of this unique ability to "ambulate" into procession, she is perceived as not only a static force of good but also a dynamic force of checkmate in human affairs.

This complexity of meaning gives the study of La Conquistadora its extraordinary interest: she is not only a figure of personal prayer and private intercession, but she also has transcended that role to gain a public role as a powerful symbol of public beneficence. This dichotomy gives her a unique stature worthy of examination.

2

Her Genesis

And who art thou sad shade?

Gigantic, visionary, thyself a visionary,

With majestic limbs and pious beaming eyes,

Spreading around with every look of thine a golden world,

Enhuing it with gorgeous hues.

—Walt Whitman, "Passage to India"

*Since the day I came, I have never been consigned to an attic or a
storeroom;*

I have always been in the midst of my people,

in their joys as well as in their sorrows—yes, even in battle.

—Fray Angélico Chávez, *Autobiography of an Ancient Statue*

To begin our study, we must know La Conquistadora's official description. It is generally accepted that her original liturgical or church-title was meant to represent the Assumption of Our Lady to Heaven, although some early descriptions reference the Annunciation or the Immaculate Conception. Her pedestal base, adorned with the faces of three cherubs, certainly matches the Assumption story (declared doctrine by Pope Pius XII in 1950) in which the Virgin Mother ascends to heaven and is crowned as Queen. Later iterations of her name in church literature reference: "Our Lady of the Rosary," "La Conquistadora," and finally, "Our Lady of Peace."

"Our Lady of the Assumption" was not a static title; in fact, within the short space of fifty years after arriving in the state, she was rechristened with various Marian titles before she became most-commonly known as "*Nuestra Señora La Conquistadora.*" This Spanish name literally means "Our Lady, the Conqueror." The verb "conquistar" means both to conquer and to win one's affections, and contains a literal reference to her in her role as "The Conqueror"—a title conferred on her by don Diego de Vargas, conquistador of old Santa Fe when the Spanish retook the city thirteen years after the Pueblo Revolt of 1680. She represented Mary's patronage and protection of the colonial city, and the de Vargas legend rests on the premise that he specifically invoked her aid in the reconquest of 1693.

None of her titles were permanent, and they were translated differently over time. So although the image also known as "*Nuestra Señora del Rosario*" could keep her title for centuries at a time, its definition would shift with the times, reflecting Santa Fe's reputation as a site of blending of cultures. For example, heated cultural debate led to a challenge of the official version of the so-called "peaceful" reconquest of Santa Fe after the Pueblo Revolt of 1680, which in turn led to her rechristening as "*Nuestra Señora de la Paz,*" represented variously in church literature as "Our Lady of Peace" or as "Conqueror of Hearts."

In addition to an official description, the statue's official parents must be part of her provenance. While her maker's name is lost to history, and her biblical parents are well known, La Conquistadora, in her contemporary existence, had many god-parents, as it were: Fray Angélico Chávez (1910–1996) and Pedro Ribera-Ortega (1931–2003) on the paternal side and, on the maternal side, the scores of women who have cared for her sacred image, often in quiet and unassuming ways. Chávez, a Franciscan priest, author, and artist has been described by professor and author Ellen McCracken as a New Mexico Renaissance man. Ribera-Ortega was a Santa Fe author, teacher, and life-long devotee of La Conquistadora. These two men did more than anyone else to fix La Conquistadora's star in the firmament of heavenly icons, and their efforts to resurrect her role in private worship and public function are nothing less than extraordinary. However, the role women have played in La Conquistadora's story cannot be underestimated, so that too will be explored in detail.

Escaping the Pueblo Revolt of 1680 is only one of the many journeys and adventures La Conquistadora has endured. Even her very "birth" at time of manufacture, evokes a sense of danger and intrigue. Finding the true facts of La Conquistadora's early existence, however, is hampered by two problems. First, there are long periods of time in which no church records exist because of destruction in the Pueblo Revolt or relatively dormant stretches between 1697 and 1777. The second problem lies in the propensity for some church officials to speculate or to engage in embellishment in describing her condition and probable history.

In assigning an origin to La Conquistadora's very first emergence into the physical world, Fray Angélico Chávez believed that she had been made out of willow wood and described a fanciful story about the man who rescued a willow log from a fire and then carved her from the piece that he had saved. Chávez documented that he sent a sliver of wood from behind La Conquistadora's left ear to Friar Herculan Kolinski, O.F.M., an expert on wood, who in turn consulted with Dr. H. Muegel, a dendrologist at the University of Cincinnati. Their conclusion was that she was made of willow wood, and Chávez lamented the fact that willow's prevalence throughout the world meant that the statue's provenance could not be traced to Spain, Michoacán, or Guatemala as he had hoped.

Mystery still surrounds the question of what wood was used in her manufacture, because La Conquistadora's other key troubadour, Pedro Ribera-Ortega, also authorized a study of the wood that resulted in a different conclusion. Whether he was simply unaware of the willow wood study, or whether it was somehow disputed, this second study was conducted after restoration work in 1997 and 1998. Originally, an expensive analysis of the wood was contemplated, but the cost was not approved, so Ribera-Ortega took wood shavings from a tiny hole that had been drilled into La Conquistadora's back and had them privately analyzed, unbeknownst to others. The analysis postulated that the sample was olive wood. He then saw to it that shavings from local "Russian Olive" trees were packed into the tiny hole that had been made.

For centuries, Spain has been a primary producer of olives, and, of course, olive wood. The New World did not have olive trees until they were introduced by the Spanish, so although olive trees now grow in Mexico, it is extremely unlikely that such a valuable, productive tree would have grown to maturity only to be cut down for the purpose of making a statue. Accordingly, this view would tend to corroborate the theory that La Conquistadora's most likely country of origin was Spain. Ribera-Ortega and others have theorized that she may also have come from places in the Holy Land, and from Palestine, but there is insufficient evidence to support these theories.

What should we make of these two studies? The initial willow analysis may have been incorrect, or the olive wood conclusion may have been faulty. By far the most tantalizing possibility, however, is that both studies may have been correct because the wood that was used for analysis was taken from two separate parts of her body. Certain details of her structure suggest that she was not fashioned of one single piece of wood, but may have been molded of separate pieces. She has certainly undergone major repairs during her lifespan, and may even have suffered a separation between her head and her torso at some point in her history. Only a comparison of wood from both her head and her torso would answer this question definitively. Further, if the wood is of two different types and the age of the wood is from different time periods, new questions about that circumstance would have dramatic implications. She may have undergone a calamity in battle or in transit across the sea, meaning that one part of her was cobbled together with a new component of a separate provenance. Alternatively, her original designer may have planned to construct her out of two kinds of wood, or two separate artists collaborated on her creation. If she is of two different materials, this odd fact may make her symbolism further enhanced; meaning that her heart/torso (willow) and mind (olive) are fundamentally disparate.

In either case, her image had a definite artistic birthplace. Spain had a long history and custom of carving wood into holy images. Originally, such images were fashioned as robed, cloaked in wooden clothing as an integral part of their figure. Other examples of images in Spain from the same era as La Conquistadora reveal that the maker had the ability to perform intricate tooling work, upon which gilding was overlaid to simulate flowing cloth. With the rise of Spain's power and wealth, such techniques gave way to a new custom of using actual cloth to dress or cloak religious figures, mirroring fashions in the sixteenth and seventeenth century royal court. The divide between the classes may have been visibly underscored by the opulent and luxurious garments that common man would not have an opportunity to see, had it not been for the public display of regal robes on a religious figure in church or procession.

We now know that La Conquistadora originally bore integral wooden robes and that her head was partially covered by a wooden hood or veil, which Chávez described as an "Oriental scarf" wrapped across her breast, with a lovely large folded mantle that dropped lightly down from her head to her feet. All the carved garments, he supposed, were then covered with smooth plaster, which was then painted crimson and covered with gold leaf. On this golden surface were traced tiny scrolled and ribbed designs, arabesques in red, orange, and blue. He fancied that this unique dress was not a classic religious or royal style, but rather the costume of a "Moorish princess" who once brightened the halls of the Alhambra, in Granada, Andalucía, truly the dress of a "Lady Palestine."

The image's modern restorations in 1930 and again in 1997–1998 reveal that many of the original wooden robes had been carved or scraped away centuries earlier. She endured a radical transformation of being divested of her wooden robes, and, in keeping with the fashion of the times, was dressed in garments that linked her immediately to the people around her and their fashions. A major question still unanswered about her transition from completely wooden figure to one that "wears" cloth is when this transformation took place. It is not known in what exact state La Conquistadora came to New Mexico, but Chávez's discovery of a receipt indicated that she already had garments when she was brought to Santa Fe in 1626, meaning that she was no longer intact or obscured by wooden veils or robe and hence could be clothed in different attire as the occasion dictated.

Being shorn of the wooden robes was not the only transformation that La Conquistadora underwent in her early existence. She has often been described as being in a state requiring triage. Chávez described La Conquistadora's original pose as "two slender hands folded before her breast." Tresses of hair showed slightly above her brow and at the sides of her neck beneath her ears, but when her mantle was scraped away, her head was reshaped to allow for wigs and crowns to be attached. Her face was inclined upward, indicating the Assumption of Mary into Heaven. But Chávez notes her height of twenty-eight inches from crown of head to feet represented a reduction in size from the original, which was approximately thirty-three inches. The top of her skull bears a hole that has been plugged with a metal brace. Her arms have been altered, "broken" to swing free, dangling at her sides, with some of her fingers broken off. Her right knee, once bent in supplication, has been shaved, making her appear erect. Her ears have been manipulated to allow for earrings to be affixed to her head. Her face of *yeso* (gesso) was brittle and peeling away before its restoration.

Explanations vary for her radical transformations over the centuries. Ribera-Ortega mused that she was whittled to fit in a crate for transport from Mexico City to Santa Fe, and theorized that the jostling of cart travel over bumpy rudimentary roads required boxing of all items in rigid fashion to withstand the rigors of the journey. Chávez, however, found documentation of the dimensions of the crate that protected her on the way to Santa Fe, and his research in the church records from the late 1600s and from 1777 made him confident that she was not altered solely for the journey from Mexico. Chávez theorized that she had been sawed off of her base of clouds below the cherubs to fit into a *nicho,* and the statue bears evidence of such sawing through the cherubs' faces, which has been subsequently repaired. Other possibilities have been suggested. The change to the knee could have been the result of a deliberate artistic decision to make her appear less as a supplicant and instead more erect, meaning that she would no longer be looking upward to her anticipated arrival in heaven. Or the change could have been to make her appear more accessible to her subjects. There are oft-repeated tales that she was either altered for the difficult journey to the New World (by ship and then by *carreta*) or to allow her to be dressed in proper attire or to hold the infant Jesus.

Unfortunately, La Conquistadora's many early transformations were not always at the hands of artists. Chávez described the changes as a kind of butchery. Fortunately, work done by the artist Gustave Baumann in 1930 and by artisan Mark Humenick in the late 1990s helped to restore her former grandeur. Baumann re-wired the articulated arms, which had been in broken pieces, and performed other general restorative work. In 1933, he also made a replica of La Conquistadora in what was supposed to be her original pose of the Assumption, which is discussed below.

Humenick's work began in 1997, when special permission was obtained to take La Conquistadora to St. Francis Elementary School, to instruct the Catholic school children in the story of the Assumption and to undertake a devotional, ceremonial crowning of her image. It was there that parishioner Nicolás St. Arnaud noticed that the putty around the base was disintegrating and separating the base from the image. Because of the passage of time since the 1930s when Baumann conducted the first restoration, the image was overdue for a makeover.

La Cofradía hired Humenick to work on the separating base, which had also been repaired before at Los Alamos by Fray Angélico Chávez's father, probably in 1948. Ribera-Ortega recounted how Humenick studied the base and took it apart, and it was then, while her image had been removed from its base, that her interior core was examined and a complete assessment of her exterior was undertaken. This second modern restoration in the 1990s allowed for science to peer into her history. Lighted scopes were used to peer into the chamber of her interior that had been carved out to allow the pole to be used. In 1998, with permission of the Archdiocese and then-*mayordomo*, Ribera-Ortega, Humenick sent a small piece of the wood from her back to the University of Arizona for study. A dendrology examination reflected a probable date range of origin between 1448 and 1648. Humenick recommended paint-chip analysis, but Ribera-Ortega had hoped to use church art experts in Spain. He passed away before this could be accomplished.

The implications of these findings for La Conquistadora's date of origin are extremely significant, although the window of two hundred years does not definitively fix her birth date. La Conquistadora could not have come from New Mexico, as olive trees do not survive in the state. Further, because there is a "chain-of-custody" to the person who brought her from Mexico City, we know that she came up the Royal Road. But because her origin possibly pre-dates her arrival in Santa Fe by two hundred years or more, she came to us with an indecipherable past. The traditional theory, that she came to the Royal City of the Holy Faith via ship from Spain, has had to compete with other theories about her origin. Although she has blue eyes, some believe that her features echo traces of people from the Holy Land. Since olive wood was also available in Portugal and the Middle East, some have theorized that her maker was not of Spanish origin but was perhaps a Catholic convert from another culture who paid homage to his homeland. Still others have proposed that the maker was of Spanish lineage but was away from his Mother country at the time of her manufacture, perhaps on a long pilgrimage, and that her distinctive features reflected the novel faces of the country he visited.

Her origins may have been lost, but there is no doubt that icons of the Virgin Mary were often a part of pilgrimages and explorations. There may have been a specific industry devoted to manufacturing traveling saints; making them portable, lightweight, and sturdy. Such an image could be used for many purposes, and could be repaired or adapted as needed. Whether it was originally a man of the cloth who selected the figure of La Conquistadora or had her made for a specific journey, or whether she was a veteran of several such journeys, or whether she was "retired" from such travails and placed on the second-hand market—these possibilities do not make her any less than her cousins who served as the titular head of an expedition. Though she eventually became more, she may have begun her existence as a distant or poor relation to the more elaborate statues in Spain, shuffled out of the way by fancier replacement images, then crated as an item of commerce, and, finally, sold to fill a church in a distant desert. What matters is that she was chosen to come to Santa Fe for a specific purpose to serve a specific church, and that her origins and subsequent history have made her an important symbol for her city.

The possibilities of her provenance lead to a discussion of the nature of the expeditions of which she became a part. The *de facto* purpose of using Spain's presence north of Mexico as a placeholder against incursions by England, France and the Netherlands meant that the mission was in essence a long-term gamble. But the approach was not completely military. The Spanish exploration consisted of two essential factions: the secular component and the religious retinue. The conquistador, often under a specific contract with the crown to furnish an expedition in exchange for a share in the fruits of the outcome, had to front the money for the enterprise. If he borrowed on his possessions in New Spain, or from family, then he was under extreme pressure to make the expedition bear fruit, so to speak, as an investment. Given the stark reality of the high desert of New Mexico, this made these explorers into big-time gamblers. In contrast, the Franciscans saw their mission as one of conversion, to save new souls. Often, these two objectives caused deep internal clashes within the expedition. The leader often had to obtain permission from the clergy in order to undertake a military campaign against the indigenous people.

The brutal landscape of New Mexico became a graveyard of the hopes and dreams of many of the Spanish explorers, from Coronado forward, and the crown's expense in this new endeavor was great, estimated at one million pesos between 1609 and 1680 alone. At times the viceroy in Mexico signaled to the crown in Spain that the entire enterprise was lost and that it should be abandoned. However, the saving grace that prevented this desertion was that every debate always stalled on the question of what to do those already converted—some estimates were as high as two thousand—so moving these people to Mexico would have been prohibitively expensive. This debate shifted the balance of power to the clergy, creating a *custodia*, and, in essence, demoting the military to a form of protection for the missionaries instead of allowing the military to rule the purpose of each conquest.

The Franciscans carried crucifix and *santo* into the remote reaches of the West. The founding of La Villa Real de la Santa Fé de San Francisco de Asís, loosely assigned to 1610, suggests the combination of military and religious authority. Don Pedro de Peralta, *El Adelantado y Primer Gobernador*, the first royal governor of New Mexico, returned to New Mexico with the Royal Banner of *Nuestra Señora de los Remedios* (of help and ransom) and with the coat of arms of *El Rey Felipe Segundo, El Rey Prudente*. Once Santa Fe was established, its needs were furnished by an extraordinary system, the mission supply service, consisting of a caravan every three to five years, commencing in Mexico City and winding through Zacatecas, Durango, Parral, and then along the Río Grande. The trip took approximately six months, and once they arrived in Santa Fe, much time was taken to distribute the cargo, make repairs, and reassemble the needed accoutrements for the return journey. The caravans were said to consist of thirty-two wagons, drawn by eight-mule teams. Each wagon could have carried as much as two tons of mission and church supplies, including hardware, altar items, clothing, and even luxury items. In return, New Mexico sent hides, blankets, and piñon nuts. Later, flocks of sheep and their Native shepherds were sent southward to be sold to the miners of New Spain.

Ribera-Ortega cites the legend that our icon of the Virgin was brought by oxen, which was likely true as mules needed more water for the long circuitous trail of the mission supply service. Franciscan Friar Alonso de Benavídes, an administrator in the mission system, began the arduous journey back to Santa Fe in late 1625, arriving in 1626. Whether she was sent specifically to the New World with specific job duties or whether Benavídes went to Mexico City window-shopping for an image, we cannot be certain. If he did have a list of requirements, she would have fit the bill. To begin with, as a representation of Our Lady of the Assumption, she would match the namesake of the *parróquia* in Santa Fe. Secondly, her small stature (approximately thirty inches in height) would have been an advantage for the difficult journey northward on the long trail of 1200 miles up *El Camino Real* ("The Royal Road"). Lastly, if she "came with papers," so to speak, by having a provenance of pilgrimage or crusade, such credentials would have been held in high regard in Catholic lore. Given the fact that the Spanish were exploring the New World, many of them must have felt as if they were on a pilgrimage of their own, and her history would mirror theirs. The example of her suffering would have done much to inspire those lost in the land that de Vargas had described as "remote beyond compare."

Thus Santa Fe, at its crossroads on major trails linking East to West (the Santa Fe Trail, Route 66) and North to South (the Camino Real) has long demarcated an intersection of peoples, faiths, and cultures. It is fitting that the city's venerable cathedral, St. Francis of Assisi, is named after a saint known for his own pilgrimages.

In either case, we are fortunate that Friar Benavídes, an accomplished scholar who wrote reports on colonial New Mexico, was her first "godfather," so to speak, taking care to record her auspicious arrival in Santa Fe on January 25, 1626.

3

A Santa Fe Thanksgiving

Some men change only the skies above them,

and not their lives,

when they run across the sea.

—Cato

¡Que viva la Fiesta!

New Mexico has been a battleground for conflicts between nations, and the state has been at the forefront of societal change in race relations and cultural paradigm shifts that are perhaps best scrutinized by looking at the phenomenon of Santa Fe through the microscope of the celebrations surrounding La Conquistadora and her central myth, that she interceded in the Reconquest of Santa Fe, creating a bloodless takeover that restored the Spanish to rule. This central myth is not true; there were casualties, but the overarching message of the fiesta celebration—that of cultural harmony— has infiltrated the collective subconscious with impressive thoroughness.

When the Spanish originally came to what is now New Mexico, they encountered a region that was in their view desolate, perhaps, but by no means empty. It was populated by several different groups of Native Americans, many of whom lived in organized, governed settlements that the Spanish called *Pueblos*, meaning villages. Although the Spanish ruled the Pueblos harshly at times, the two cultures lived in relative peace for many years. Some Natives accepted the Catholic religion that the missionaries brought, many maintained their traditional beliefs, and others adopted a mixture of the two faiths.

In the 1660s and 1670s, relations between the two cultures deteriorated. A religious leader named Po'pay, along with other pueblo leaders, organized a revolt, attacking the Spanish in widely separated settlements on a single day. By August 21, 1680, the siege on Santa Fe had broken the resolve of the Spanish, and they retreated southward to San Lorenzo and Santísimo Sacramento, also known as El Paso del Norte, near the modern El Paso. Any hope for a rapid reconquest of New Mexico after the Pueblo Revolt was dashed by the harsh conditions that the Spanish found themselves in at their temporary location. Conditions in San Lorenzo caused crops to fail, and the men's fatigue was exacerbated by the fear of continued attacks. In 1681, Governor don Antonio de Otermín's reconnaissance expeditions carried a message to the Native people that repentance would produce amnesty. A subsequent intense attack on Zia Pueblo by Otermín's successor, Domingo Jironza Petriz de Cruzate, perhaps paved the way for a return to Santa Fe with few casualties.

In 1691 a new man was sent to the exiles in the El Paso area, scattered as they were on both sides of the Río Grande del Norte. He was don Diego de Vargas Zapata y Luján, Ponce de Léon, whose aristocratic family hailed from Madrid. It was said that as a Spanish Grandee, he had the overbearing personality and ripe confidence necessary for undertaking a mission regarded as fraught with peril: the reconquest of the North for Spain.

De Vargas and his men started northward in September of 1692, conducting a reconnaissance mission in Santa Fe that indicated that peaceful reentry could be achieved. When he returned in full force in October of 1693, he learned of the threat of renewed Native attacks. An early winter made conditions unfavorable, and food was scarce. A tentative peace accord between the two sides disintegrated, so de Vargas was forced to convert the approach to a military one, and in the battle that ensued on December 16, 1693, blood was shed and, by most accounts, eighty-one Natives died, with seventy of that number executed upon surrender. Four hundred others were enslaved. A subsequent revolt in 1696 was quelled, and additional soldiers and settlers continued to join the battalion at Santa Fe.

La Conquistadora in the Sacristy, 2009. Photograph by the author.

From one point of view, the battle was a small event in Spain's retaking of the region, but the event has taken on legendary significance under the adage that if you repeat a story often enough, it will be considered true: it has come to mean a relatively peaceful reconquest carried out by a man who combined martial attributes with a desire for peace. The image of the Virgin figures prominently in this story and provides the basis for La Conquistadora as a symbol of cultural reconciliation. De Vargas's 1692 campaign journals indicate that his troops followed a particular Royal Standard (or banner) on which was painted the figure of the representation of *Nuestra Señora de los Remedios* ("of help and ransom"), one of the many titles under which New World Spaniards honored Mary Immaculate. De Vargas was said to be particularly attached to this image.

As Fray Angélico Chávez has noted, de Vargas's journals do not actually report that La Conquistadora went into battle; other accounts refer only to a banner with her image. Ribera-Ortega's view that de Vargas did carry her may simply be a tribute to Ribera-Ortega's enthusiasm for legend. Nevertheless, the story of her being carried into battle was persistent. Chávez also believed in La Conquistadora's military antecedents: "All this makes one suspect that the Conquistadora statue, together with the larger infant and San Miguel, might have gone into battle after all, even though documentary proof of this fact is still lacking."

Chávez passed away in 1996, but Pedro Ribera-Ortega participated in discovering new evidence in the late 1990s. During the restoration by Mark Humenick, the image was carefully lifted from her base in order to analyze how best to restore the base. It was then that Humenick discovered that the hole in the bottom of the figure indicated the presence of a pole inside, and that a piece of canvas cloth appeared to be keeping the standard pole from moving. Chávez had described the pole as "pin" used to fit the base and the statue together, but Ribera-Ortega believed it was a standard. In either case, the conclusions were that La Conquistadora had been hollowed out and that she had two back sections. Ribera-Ortega arranged for her image to be x-rayed at St. Vincent's Hospital. That procedure confirmed that she had been hollowed out, and, further, that the pole was still embedded inside her. Anecdotal evidence of pieces of a Spanish flag being embedded also lent credence to these theories. Unfortunately, although previous restorers had carefully returned the cloth to its hiding place Ribera-Ortega did not return the cloth, and knowledge of its whereabouts disappeared when he died in 2003.

Ribera-Ortega drew conclusions from these reports to support his theory that La Conquistadora had been placed on a standard pole that had been carried into Santa Fe in 1693 during what he called the "*Santa Fe Plaza de Armas*, Reconquest of de Vargas by the Second Entrada." Ribera-Ortega's *abuelita* (grandmother) doña María Catarina Sánchez de Ribera-Ortiz, told him that her grandmothers' grandmothers had carried down an oral tradition of tales of de Vargas and the reconquest of Santa Fe, and that La Conquistadora had played her role in these matters. Ribera-Ortega likened this to medieval practices of Marian images being placed on flags, or of the images themselves being carried onto the battlefield at the right of the commander, while the reins of war were at the left.

Ribera-Ortega noted that *Nuestra Señora de los Remedios* was present in other New World explorations. For example, she was also revered by Conquistador Hernán Cortés and used as a banner image in his conquest of Mexico. Ribera-Ortega believed that this practice was traceable back to Spain near Sevilla, the town Los Palacios - Villafranca de la Marisma where a Penitente Chapel of *Nuestra Señora de los Remedios* was maintained and where an annual feast, held in October, creates a town fiesta, not unlike La Conquistadora celebrations in Santa Fe, New Mexico.

The centuries-old practice of venerating saints and carrying their likenesses into processions might also have served as the reason for La Conquistadora's hollow center. Her aristocratic features may have graced a sojourn to the Crusades, in fighting for a place in the New World, or simply as an ameliorating presence after-the-fact in procession, to underscore peaceful and benign purposes for the imposition of one culture on another. The x-ray image of her indicates that the pole inclines ten degrees or so to the left, allowing for her to appear upright if carried on the right-hand side, since most people wielding her would be right-handed. Although Fray Angélico Chávez did not ascribe such fanciful reasons to what he determined was a simple structural method to connect La Conquistadora to her base, the x-ray image of the shape inside her also reveals a carved knob atop the pole, an embellishment that would not be needed if the pole's only purpose was as to hold the statue to its base. Additionally, two other holes were carved into the statue's base at ninety degree angles, indicating that the image could be adjusted depending on method of carriage; for example, by horse stirrup, by hand, or other methods. Mayodomo Ignacio Garcia believes that the incline design for the pole was deliberate, and that great care was taken to insure that her image did not lean precipitously and that her regal bearing never faltered, ever pointing straight up toward heaven.

In any case, by the time de Vargas set about to retake New Mexico, either he chose to alter her title, or she came to be known by the title that best-reflected her new purpose, and *Nuestra Señora de la Conquista* ("Our Lady of the Conquest") was born. De Vargas had chosen her image, with female connotations of peace and love to pull off a masterful and very male enterprise. In contrast, when don Juan de Oñate fought Ácoma Pueblo in 1598, the victory was attributed to the apparition of St. James riding a white horse and wielding a terrible sword, either spurring the Spanish soldiers on or frightening the Native opponents into submission. De Vargas chose a different approach, actually a fusion of approaches, bringing both armaments and ameliorating symbols at his side.

De Vargas's approach to Santa Fe was a delicate one. Initial negotiations with the natives indicated a possible peaceful takeover. He negotiated with the Tano Indians living in Santa Fe, and the Blessed Virgin's banner must have been featured prominently in the discussions. De Vargas was wise enough to know that he had to contend with two disparate elements of the Spanish incursion in the Western World; that of the mercenary soldiers seeking profits or lands, and that of the mission system, seeking converts to the Catholic faith. In order to reconcile these two factions and succeed in retaking Santa Fe, one can surmise that de Vargas must have been fully aware of the mirror elements in Native society.

Indian leaders may have had individual feelings of revenge or battle lust, while others, primarily those previously converted, or their off-spring, may have wanted to see the return of the Spanish, while still others might have just wanted to avoid bloodshed. De Vargas's successful return to Santa Fe exploited the military intelligence of the time: that reconquest might be achieved due to Popé's own cruelty, the ravages of harsh living conditions, or conflicts of faith among the Native people.

Having achieved the semblance of an agreement, De Vargas returned to El Paso to commence preparations to return to Santa Fe with the colonists. Whether De Vargas was honoring the spirit of the moment, or whether he somehow hoped to re-brand her image to burnish his own fame we will never know, but his motives did seem pure in that he frequently wrote about her, using the new terminology, for example, in reports to the viceroy in Mexico City.

The story of the reconquest of Santa Fe is not as peaceful as legend suggests. There was fighting, and lives were lost. Despite these tragedies, de Vargas is a symbol of one of the recurring themes of the La Conquistadora legend: that devotion to her is akin to the relationship between a queen and her knights. As historian Warren Beck noted, in his book, *New Mexico/ A History of Four Centuries,* de Vargas epitomized the chivalric behavior of his lineage and upbringing:

> [He was] a scion of an illustrious Spanish family distinguished by centuries of service to both church and crown. In many respects, Vargas represented the noblest ideal of the medieval Spanish knight. In him were embodied the religious fervor of Spain's reconquest of the peninsula against the Moors, the desire to do valorous deeds on the field of battle so as to be worthy of his knightly calling, and an unbelievable energy and strength of character. His courage was so great that at times it verged on the foolhardy. In his dealings with the New Mexican natives, he was at one and the same time a suave diplomat, a decisive

military leader, and a resourceful and experienced campaigner. Though always ready to fight, Vargas preferred to win his point by diplomacy. Unfortunately, this man was also to be capable of implacable cruelty toward the Indians, a trait that was to prove costly to the Spaniards in the long run. Even with this failing, Don Diego de Vargas deserves to rank with Coronado as one of the noblest Spaniards in the history of New Mexico.[1]

De Vargas spent much of his own fortune in the endeavors of exploration, only to be replaced in 1697 by don Pedro Cuberó. De Vargas was accused of cruelty to Natives and of using his office for personal enrichment. He was imprisoned for three years in *La Nueva España* (Old Mexico). When he finally laid his case before the viceroy and was cleared of these charges, he returned to Santa Fe and was appointed to another term as governor. He died in April of 1704, but after his death his legend was revised by some historians who asserted that he died from injuries sustained after helping a Pueblo defend itself from an attack by Plains Indians.

The actual facts of the battles and lives are lost to popular memory and culture. What is popularly remembered and repeated in Santa Fe lore is that de Vargas camped at a site near where Rosario Chapel now stands, and that he knelt to pray before La Conquistadora, requesting her intercession that bloodshed be avoided in reestablishing the colony for the Spanish. De Vargas is said to have vowed to build a shrine to her: "[t]hat if this conquest be made without loss of life or shedding of blood, I promise to institute in your honor, O Holy Mother of God, an annual Novena which will be observed for all time." But it was not until 1712, eight years after de Vargas' death, that an edict was issued proclaiming an annual fiesta to commemorate the bloodless reconquest. Fray Angélico Chávez noted that De Vargas donated costly items to the Cofradía de La Conquistadora, and that he was elected as mayordomo in 1692, serving successive terms. Chávez also found evidence that, despite the dearth of references in de Vargas's writings about La Conquistadora's actual presence during the reconquest, some mention in the writings of others place her at the campsite where the settlers awaited word of victory and prayed for her intercession.

Although de Vargas may not have known it then, he is now inextricably linked to La Conquistadora for all time, as the legend has replaced the event itself. De Vargas asked to be buried in La Conquistadora's chapel next to his wife, doña Teodora de Garcia de la Riva. Because the new church at that site had not been completed before he died, we cannot be certain where he is buried; either the *campo santo* north of the La Conquistadora's present-day chapel at the Basilica, or elsewhere at another parish. Some say that his wish was so great—or his descendants were so true to their promise—that he was disinterred from his first burial site and moved to the *parróquia* after 1714 so that he and his Lady of Conquest would always be together.

The period after the reconquest saw great changes in Santa Fe. While the Natives had destroyed much of the original *casas reales*, the *Barrio de Analco* across the river where San Miguel Mission ("The Oldest Church") had stood was, as housing for natives, still somewhat intact when the reconquest took place. Because the central parish church, the *parróquia*, had been destroyed, worship took place at temporary churches until the new *parróquia* could be built. The military chapel on the plaza, the *Presidio de la Santa Cruz*, grew in stature for some time as various versions of the town's houses of worship were built. It was not until 1807 that the *Capilla de Nuestra Señora del Rosario* (Rosario Chapel) was completed at the site where de Vargas is believed to have camped before reentering the city. The main parish church was rebuilt many times over the years, requiring temporary removal of La Conquistadora.

La Conquistadora was a nomad of sorts even in her own city, forced to hold court at different temporary locations while four subsequent iterations of the main cathedral were built over the centuries. Thus her legend, even from the beginning, contained the concept that she could bi-locate at will, a heavenly apparition starting on her journey to become a legend and a cultural symbol. That she would reign in the grandest edifice seemed logical, but she was also tied to Rosario Chapel by de Vargas. Her annual journey in

June from the cathedral back to Rosario, in thanksgiving as De Vargas had dictated, is a mobile symbol of her vagabond, gypsy nature, proof that she belonged to the entire spectrum of the community, not just as a symbol of the elite in a royal court, but also as an icon for the servant class, the workers, and the Native people who had accepted her.

This became one of her strongest attributes; that she had been close to her subjects from all walks of life, throughout the city, and not tied to one spot eternally. Her accessibility became a tradition. So although the church at the heart of the city became the central church, Rosario and San Miguel Mission served as figurative branches or arms of La Conquistadora's reach into the city, extending her legend into the Barrio Analco of the Natives and the encampment of the Spanish, in essence uniting the two sides.

Thus La Conquistadora began as a symbol of battle but became much more. After the Pueblo Revolt, she was the most powerful inspirational figure to motivate the men who had been in exile for twelve long years. And in a sense, her presence was as a "founder" of the city, with the ideal hope that the return would be peaceful, so that these ideals imbued her mythology with strong powers. Explorers of the New World had broken into the unknown, leaving the familiar for the uncertain. This form of transcendence led a visionary like de Vargas to venerate La Conquistadora to the exclusion of all other images. Although blood was spilled, his promised shrine was built, first a modest *jacál* of interwoven branches and later a stout edifice of adobe and artistry, and the legend took root. Many have theorized that the hardship and travail of living in the wilderness of New Mexico forced peoples to band together to survive, knitting the Old World to the New. Friction between the dominant culture and other cultures has come down through the centuries, but the pageantry, theatre, and message of Santa Fe's founding has created an entire tradition of Thanksgiving that grew up around the event now known as Fiesta de Santa Fe, an event explored in a subsequent chapter.

4

Finding Her Footing

She walks among us . . . we collapse time,

to the time when Jesus walked . . . .

—Charles M. Carrillo, Ph.D.

. . . even the dark and the light bring about a faith

that keeps our familia intact and loved and cared for and deeply,

deeply connected to la virgin/

and you knew the power of our sacred lady,

that was why you pursued your path so diligently,

to make known to the world Her love for us.

—Jimmy Santiago Baca, Poem written for the
100th birthday of Fray Angélico Chávez on April 10, 2010.

La Conquistadora's exact origins are shrouded in mystery. There are two conflicting schools of thought regarding her specific heritage. The first view is that her striking features, sometimes called "Palestinian," are the product of a romantic and mysterious origin in the Holy Land. The other view is that she was a product of a specific artist in Spain. In either case, she is a hybrid of sorts, the intersection of a cosmic mixture, with startling blue eyes. La Conquistadora's physical beginnings, however, point to her metaphorical beginnings after she arrived in the New World, for it is there that her traditional story begins and where we find the first evidence of what she has come to mean to people.

Fray Angélico Chávez did much to document the drama of La Conquistadora's story. While his belief that she had been entirely constructed out of willow wood turned out to be incorrect, his role is clear in promoting her rise to prominence in the legends and beliefs of New Mexico. Ordained as a Franciscan priest in 1937, Chávez spent time in remote parishes and must have felt the need to connect the hinterlands with the Mother Church in Santa Fe. He popularized La Conquistadora by bringing a "traveling version" to churches throughout New Mexico. La Conquistadora is not allowed to travel widely; church officials must approve her journeys. But Gustave Baumann, in conjunction with his 1930 restoration, had constructed a replica for La Conquistadora. The replica, which assumed La Conquistadora's original rigid pose of the Assumption, with arms crossed in supplication and knee bent forward in curtsy, became known as *La Peregrina*, meaning "the pilgrim," or traveler. Chávez began to take La Peregrina on pilgrimages, carrying her to some 95 churches throughout northern New Mexico. It is difficult to gauge to what extent her presence in so many places may have contributed to her legendary status, but certainly, especially prior to the information age's control of the public imagination, ambient awareness of her presence in these far-flung communities must have created a network of family-style discussions, stories, and anecdotes about her visits. Chávez's storytelling ability and his scholarship in documenting the journey that brought her to New Mexico resonated with many who had made their own journeys to the state.

Pedro Ribera-Ortega assumed the mantle of responsibility for La Conquistadora when Chávez passed away in 1996. It is at this point in her history that we see an expansion of information added to burnish her legend. Originally, Ribera-Ortega's writings reflected the popular belief that because her image was not purely European in mien, she must have originated in the medieval context of a crusade or an artist returning from pilgrimage in the Holy Land. Ribera-Ortega began extensive travels to Spain and to Mexico, but found few images that resembled La Conquistadora in any way. His writings reflect that he initially attributed this lack of similar images to the fact that she had been crafted in a Palestinian style, or by someone of non-Spanish descent. This theory corroborated, in his view, his belief in her power as a tool of conversion.

Certainly this theory held great appeal across a broad spectrum of New Mexicans because their own stories of immigration to the New World were cloaked in disguise or mystery. Refugees of all sorts found their way to New Mexico, sometimes as legitimate parts of an official group, but just as often as not, fleeing the Spanish Inquisition, penal banishment, or as a *converso* or Sephardic Jew. Others came in military service, church service, or in an administrative capacity. Cut off from La Tierra Madre, in alien territory, these lost ones, separated from their families, found someone to cling to in the figure of La Conquistadora, and the story of her crusading past resonated with their inner longings.

Ribera-Ortega continued his research in many directions, with each new discovery providing him with additional reason to revisit La Conquistadora's mythology. For example, when it was discovered that she was made out of olive wood (which we now know may only be her torso), he analyzed how olive wood and olive oil factor into the Catholic religion. He referred to the Old Testament, and cited instances where olive oil is used in religious and holy purposes and in the cuisine of Spain and Palestine. He noted as well the oil's use in various sacraments of the Catholic Church—for example, the three kinds of olive oil that bishops consecrate and bless during Holy Week of Lent for the use in the sacraments of Baptism, Confirmation, and Services for the Sick and Dying. To Ribera-Ortega, that La Conquistadora's maker should choose to craft her of olive wood was a symbolic act of profound significance. He may have intuited that an ancient tree represents growth and development of psychic life, hence the olive tree used to make La Conquistadora's torso links us to the deepest layers of the collective unconscious and takes us mentally to the sacred places that sustain life.

Consuelo Hernández caring for La Conquistadora's garments in 1950. Photograph by Laura Gilpin, Private Collection, Untitled, 1950, Gelatin Silver Print, © Amon Carter Museum , Fort Worth, Texas.

In his later years, Ribera-Ortega seemed to change his thinking about La Conquistadora's origin. He made over twelve trips to Spain, and many to Mexico City, continuing to collect material; he saw hundreds if not thousands of images of Mary. Only once, he said, did he see an image similar to La Conquistadora: when he was in Sevilla, and possibly once in an ancient church in Salamanca. In Sevilla, Ribera-Ortega found what he believed was an almost identical image of Our Lady of the Rosary at the famous fifteenth century Hospital de la Caridad. The church was built by Miguel Mañara, who divested himself of two large fortunes from his Italian and Spanish ancestors and devoted himself to *Caridad Cristiana para los pobres y los moribundos*, also known as the Apostolate of the Sick and Dying and Burial of the Dead Poor. The fact that the Sevilla image dated to the fourteenth century suggested to Ribera-Ortega that his own statue was likewise just as old. Ribera-Ortega later changed his theory to the belief that she was made by someone of Spanish heritage.

La Conquistadora's countenance was sufficiently unusual to have traces of all peoples, so she spoke to all peoples. As Mark Humenick noted during his restoration work, her expression seemed to change on a frequent basis. Furthermore, La Conquistadora was a traveler, like her subjects. In consultation with Spanish colleagues, Ribera-Ortega espoused the theory that La Conquistadora was packed onto a Spanish galleon out of Sevilla to Vera Cruz, Mexico, and from there to México (under the Aztecs, Tenochitlán), the capital of Nueva España, where she came to the attention of Benavídes, who in turn brought her north to Santa Fe. Because Ribera-Ortega found that her physical size was smaller in stature than similar images in Spain, he proposed that she was intended to journey into battle. Others have suggested that she was intended for export to the New World as part of the battery of proselytizing tools. In any case, she was always destined to be a traveler. She traveled not only physically but also symbolically as she has undergone various transformations. Paradoxically, her very travels have allowed her shrine in Santa Fe to solidify as a spiritual base. The tradition of her malleability helps her endure because she always reflects the times and is a product of her people and their varying projections upon her.

La Conquistadora's flexible meanings, however, have not been sufficient to resolve all the conflicts of the region where she resides. Santa Fe's actual history is not a benign story of love, peace, and understanding, a subject explored in a subsequent chapter. The conflict between the First Nations and the dominant culture has not achieved ultimate or final resolution, and clashes between people and cultures persist to this day. Further, internecine feuds and rivalries plague certain families as well. For La Conquistadora to survive this tumultuous history is a testament to her adaptability as a symbol.

La Conquistadora travels very rarely. The rules for her travel are that only the Archdiocese and the Basilica Rector can allow her to leave her chapel, aside from her annual procession to Rosario Chapel and a Fiesta-related event. Care is taken not to allow her to be made part of secular celebrations or parades; La Conquistadora's heavenly descent from her shrine to be carried in procession is a carefully scripted and controlled event. This dichotomy between her public persona and her private one has helped make her an enduring icon, preserving her mystique and magical qualities. There are many symbols of Santa Fe—some, unfortunately co-opted by commercial interests. Much to-do about the famous "blend of cultures" in the Royal City has made it so that no single symbol can bear the entire spectrum of values the City represents. However, no other symbol besides La Conquistadora comes close to capturing so much of the public imagination.

The power of her symbolism is evident in the Fiesta celebrations that merge secular parties with religious ceremony, and as La Conquistadora makes her way out the front door of the Basilica to her temporary shrine at Rosario Chapel, she attains universal stature as a cultural by-product of syncretism. In its broadest definition, "syncretism" means the combination or reconciliation of differing beliefs in religion, philosophy, and so on. In Santa Fe, this is perfectly demonstrated by the annual Fiesta event. The entire Fiesta celebration is composed of various pageants that reiterate the central myth of a peaceful reunification of the City, with various historic characters portrayed by local citizens: don Diego de Vargas and his *cuadrilla*, a generic "Queen" and her court, including "Indian Princesses" and Franciscan friars.

Their numerous appearances throughout the city and state are seen by literally thousands of people, and parades and parties surround the event. Carefully scripted dramatizations of the interaction of cultures are crafted to underscore a reconciliation theme.

La Conquistadora and her "avatar" La Peregrina are venerated by the faithful and admired by many people of all different faiths, or of no faith. Many native New Mexicans find roots of many peoples in their family trees, and as Pedro Ribera-Ortega is said to have told friends, he knew he was part "Indio" due to his ancestral home's origins in the old Barrio de Analco part of town, where the natives and servants originally lived. The Fiesta celebrants come from each sector of the community, and many people trace their family heritage back to a blend of conqueror and the conquered. La Cofradía catalogues the bird feathers left in her chapel by Native Americans and keeps archives of the thousands of good wishes sent to her annually from around the world.

How La Conquistadora came to be identified as a unifying force and purveyor of peace is traceable to three primary forces: La Cofradía de la Conquistadora, the *parróquia* that later became the St. Francis Cathedral Basilica, and the very people of Santa Fe. During the City's 400th anniversary celebrations in 2009 and in 2010, the Catholic faithful held a parallel *cuarto-centenario* celebration honoring the church's history.

In examining the mythology of La Conquistadora, we must compile all the instances of the miracle of her longevity, but without blinders that would cloud or obscure the entire story of her legend. The entirety of her legend must be looked at: not only the divine but also the mundane, corporeal facts of her existence in order to have a true picture.

5

Beyond Above

En el portal de Belén

Los gitanos se congregant.

San José, lleno de heridas,

Amortaja a una doncella . . . .

(In the doorway of Bethlehem

the gypsies congregate.

Saint Joseph, full of wounds,

enshrouds the maiden . . . .)

—Federico García Lorca

Truth will not stand or stay or keep . . . it is either new or not at all.

—Norman O. Brown

Even in ancient times, priestesses such as the Greek Sibyl were able to communicate with the gods and transform the inscrutable into divine will. As religion became a way to consolidate power, this individual approach was abandoned, altering the archetypal female at one with nature to a cloistered Virgin, sublime and pure. This new female archetype was all positive in her attributes, so that any popular beliefs in dark magic were cast aside, as were all links to gypsies, witches and any other practitioners of the so-called dark arts. In Christianity, Mary became the ideal to which all must subscribe in order to avoid eternal damnation. Parallels to Mary are found in other cultures, in China, the goddess Kwan-Yin; in India, Shakti, Parvati, Rati, and others; and among the Muslims, Fatima, the daughter of Mohammed. Spanish cultural heritage is suffused with the image of the Virgin Mary, and her reach is evident in the replication of her image throughout Christian history and world cultures. She is called by many names: but with one theme, that she is a redemptive instrument of divine love, unique among the saints.

Thousands of representations of Mary—Our Lady of Fatima, Our Lady of Lourdes, and Our Lady of Guadalupe, and many more—create a central mythology of Mary as a heavenly apparition, able to bi-locate and send messages to the faithful. These stories provide the background for La Conquistadora. The mystery and romance of her own journey to Santa Fe add their own flavor, and the collection of stories about La Conquistadora has now become legend.

While our knowledge of La Conquistadora's history is subject to the vagaries of her caregivers' archives and the frailty of human memory, she has been the subject of a large number of ritual events, most witnessed by the public; the number of annual masses, novenas, and spiritual quests is stunning. Thus any history of La Conquistadora must take a two-fold approach. There is the statue, and then there are the stories of those affected by her. She is imbued with human experience, and her handlers and devotees make choices that will resonate long after they are gone.

For example, at some point in time, she began to carry *Santa Niño de*

Atocha, a Christ child: adding to her mystery as a symbol, but underscoring her value as a malleable namesake that could adapt with the times and with what might be perceived as necessary for a given situation. One story about Santo Niño involves Jean Baptiste Lamy, who served the Santa Fe region as Bishop (appointed in 1850, arriving in 1851) and then Archbishop (when the Diocese became an Archdiocese in 1875) until 1888. When the nearby *Santuario de Chimayo* church gained a reputation for the healing powers of its holy dirt, Archbishop Lamy was said to have taken the Santo Niño statue from Chimayo to the cathedral. Folklore held, however, that the little saint kept making his way back to Chimayo because he did not like the cathedral, and that explained why his little moccasins were repeatedly worn out even though new pairs were left for him.

The practice of carrying her in procession to Rosario Chapel was first held in 1771 when she was proclaimed patroness of New Mexico. Now held annually on the Sunday after Corpus Christi, the procession has given rise to many anecdotes. Ribera-Ortega recounted a legend concerning the return procession, the so-called Second Procession Sunday, when La Conquistadora was brought back from Rosario Chapel to the *Parróquia* where the cathedral is today. Fray Angélico Chávez estimated her weight at approximately twenty pounds, and her palanquin would be an additional weight. However, the legend detailed how her image would become "much heavier" and only with great difficulty could she be carried the some three miles of the return journey from Rosario Chapel. Great lightning storms would also occur on the Second Procession Sunday as well. These difficulties were taken as signs that Our Lady did not want to leave the parish and its pastors, and that they should be given more days of a second Novena. This situation led to the modern practice of having a Double Novena, a Mass in the early morning and a 5:15 PM mass for devotees who wished a second service.

Fray Angélico Chávez saw procession and pilgrimage as close to the heart of La Conquistadora's meaning for the people. He believed that the custom when leaving Mexico City to travel to Santa Fe was to stop at Tepeyac Hill and venerate *La Tilma de la Virgin Santísima de Guadalupe,* with Mass said there before the long trip north on the *Camino Real de Tierra Adentro*. La Conquistadora's original journey to Santa Fe, which began in 1625 and brought her to her destination in 1626, would have made such a stop, he suggested. The custom of pilgrimage and worship in the Hispanic culture was so pronounced that even the symbol herself reenacts the symbolic customs, wearing the tradition into the fabric of culture in such a profound way that it can almost be said to reside in the genetic structure of the state's people.

Part of the custom of the procession involves accessibility to people of all walks of life. Ribera-Ortega describes the legend from the 1850s surrounding La Conquistadora and doña Gertrudis Barceló, a famous courtesan and gambler known as *La Tules* or *doña Tules*. Tules was said to have great private devotion to La Conquistadora. Processions would often pass her establishment, causing some of her "girls" to solicit parade-goers or Cofradía officers to take "refreshment" at the Tules saloon. This situation caused the nuns and other women who carried La Conquistadora great consternation, given the nature of the establishment that Tules ran. They protested that the parade should not go nearby. As they would approach her place of business, however, the statue would become very heavy, almost impossible to move. The officers of the Cofradia interpreted this heaviness to mean that La Conquistadora did not mind the short delay for refreshment, and that she in fact consented to the practice. There is no proof of this legend, but it is interesting to note that Tules was the first woman to be buried at the cathedral, and that she paid funds to Lamy to secure such an honor, as described by historian Mary J. Straw Cook in her book, *Doña Tules/Santa Fe's Courtesan and Gambler*.

La Conquistadora's role as a symbol of the common people continues into modern times. When her traveling replica La Peregrina made the journey to Spain in 1993, she was not taken to visit royalty as an exclusive object of veneration worthy only of the elite. Instead, she visited Santa Fe's sister city, Santa Fé de la Vega, and a unique Gypsy Mass was held in her honor. Consuelo Hernández recalled the gypsies singing and dancing for her in the Spanish church.

As La Peregrina, La Conquistadora can travel more widely and participate in secular events and situations. Some of her visits can be interpreted as calculated to make statements on issues of the day. For example, in 1996, she was taken to the Ground Zero Nuclear Test Site at White Sands Missile Range, near White Sands National Monument. Photographer Craig Varjabedian took photographs of her at the stone marker known as "Trinity Site" and he recounts the extraordinary circumstances surrounding the event. Previous peace vigils held at the gates to the mostly-closed site called for delicate negotiations to obtain access, which Archbishop Michael J. Sheehan oversaw. There was some fear of possible difficulty, and the cars of those in the delegation, including the blue Cadillac bearing La Peregrina, were searched upon arrival. Varjabedian recollects his feelings that she was a statement of peace and that her alternate persona as a conqueress was juxtaposed against J. Robert Oppenheimer's reference to the Bhagavad-Gita, in which Krishna is attempting to convince the Prince that he should do his duty: "I am become death, the destroyer of worlds." The group of women accompanying her had been up late the night before, carefully selecting her garments and dressing her for the occasion, and her safety on this mission was utmost in everyone's mind. Former sacristana Consuelo Hernández believes that the mission helped to ameliorate some of the turmoil surrounding the development of the atom bomb, and the somber feelings of that day paid tribute to the loss of innocence the bomb symbolizes. Varjabedian recalls that La Peregrina was carried on someone's lap for the long drive from Santa Fe, and how the concern for her was palpable among those assembled.

As the delegation was leaving, Varjabedian realized to his dismay that the photos he had taken were set at the wrong exposure. There was no way to return because the gates had been closed. However, when he got back to Santa Fe, he developed the film immediately, and found that not all the shots had been ruined; one was sufficiently light. He says that he tends to want to believe that this circumstance may have been the result of her divine plan, and that if she chose to open the clouds for one instant only, the reason behind that illumination must be respected.

La Conquistadora (Our Lady of Peace) at the Trinity Nuclear Test Site, near Socorro, New Mexico, 1996. Photograph © Craig Varjabedian.

In Pueblo culture, dress for purposes of a sacred dance requires gathering of the material over the left shoulder, as gathering on the right symbolizes death. In Varjabedian's photograph, La Peregrina is on the left. Aesthetically, her regal cape eerily mirrors the triangular outline of the stone memorial to which she was adjacent, and her image glows with light that the stone edifice matches with darkness. The alien landscape, with distant wire fence, mountain range, and clouds, evokes what a celestial home would become if everything heavenly was marooned in a lunar crater.

La Conquistadora's most profound influences, however, have been perhaps on individuals, one at a time. The prayer request book at the Cathedral is not open to inspection, but anecdotal evidence indicates that people travel from all over the world in a steady stream to see her. In the context of human experience, prayer is meant to be a private and personal journey, and most devotees are reluctant to discuss how she has intervened in their life. But we do have some clues as to her effect on people.

On the question of what artists describe as "blood memory" or ancestral memory, Roswell resident Josephine Gutiérrez speaks of how her job duties in Santa Fe during the 1950s required her to make daily visits to the United States Post Office. She found herself repeatedly visiting La Conquistadora Chapel as often as she could. Years after she retired, she began a genealogical study of her family tree and discovered that her great-great-great-great-great-great-great grandmother was the woman who had rescued La Conquistadora during the Pueblo Revolt of 1680, Josefa López Sambrano de Grijalva.

Film maker E. Anthony Martinez spoke about his experience making the documentary *El Corazón de Santa Fe*. In 2007 and 2008, he had spent thousands of dollars and made many trips between Dallas, Texas and Santa Fe trying to secure funding for a movie about Santa Fe to celebrate the 400th anniversary in 2010. Many meetings and discussions over two long years had been fruitless, and he resolved to stop trying, but he stopped into La Conquistadora Chapel on his last visit and prayed to her image. As he left the building, he encountered Basilica officials who were looking for a film maker, and the film became a reality.

These experiences perhaps suggest that La Conquistadora has had a profound effect upon those who spend time with her, who have tended her, who have protected her. Many of the names of the women and men who have tended to her over the centuries will never be known; some of their stories are told in a subsequent chapter. But personal changes can happen even when they are not expected. When Gustave Baumann undertook her restoration in the 1930s, he was said to have become so enamored of her features that it was then that he offered to make the replica, La Peregrina. Baumann, with his fame as a maker of marionettes, could have produced a soulless giant puppet, but he clearly experienced his own transformation in working on her. His efforts contributed to the transition of La Conquistadora from a frozen statue to a figure with mobility and movement, in a sense, bringing her to life and, as La Peregrina, bringing her to people far and wide.

Fray Angélico Chávez communed with La Conquistadora in startling depth. In true Santa Fe "new age" fashion, he channeled her in writings and purported to act as a scribe of her own story. Author Luis Leal discusses Chávez's work *La Conquistadora: Autobiography of an Ancient Statue* as follows:

> Readers, of course, accept the omniscient nature of the statue, since from the beginning, as in all fables, they have suspended their belief in admitting that the statue can talk . . . . The fictitious element in the book—letting a wooden statue be the narrator—has the function of an esthetic frame, in which novelistic discourse is used in order to make the history of New Mexico, from the early seventeenth century to the middle of the nineteenth century as interesting as possible.[2]

The result was effective, Leal maintains, because "Often fiction and history blend to create a new dimension. In 'La Conquistadora' historical facts are intermingled with the statue's personal observations to give the narrative verisimilitude."[3]

Pedro Ribera-Ortega likewise came under La Conquistadora's spell. Although his focus was devoted to her scientific study and to the inventory of countless images of saints in Spanish churches as he sought to discover her origins, he, too, had a strong emotional and spiritual connection to her. Each fact, each piece of evidence, each legend that he gathered he imbued with deep meaning. One might say that as mayordomo and home-grown scholar, he furthered both her history and her legend even as he lived his life in unfailing devotion to her.

Such deep personal transformation may not be possible for all, but La Conquistadora has had a place in the life of many. In any audience with the queen, there can be no prayer without both a maker and a receiver. There can be no transformative experience without both halves of the experience: the giver or "maker" of the experience and the listener, the recipient. The veracity of what is experienced is in a way irrelevant; as Marshall McLuhan would say, the medium is the message. The fact that she can be all things to all people, that she contains multitudes, is what contributes to her legendary status.

Although the walls of La Conquistadora's chapel are not lined with crutches, the legend of her power is strong. In reaching the Father and the Holy Spirit, she is the mechanism that triangulates faith, even if she is not part of the Holy Trinity. Believers thus describe La Conquistadora as the "co-redemptrix" with a powerful draw due to her proximity to Christ. While dogma or doctrine may divide followers into sects, orders, or churches, they see Mary as a unifying force, one with a kind of power not borne of words or doctrine, but instead as a powerful image, something seen. For those who honor and venerate her, "seeing is believing," the truncated version of the medieval axiom "seeing is believing, but to touch [is] the Word of God."

6

The Light Behind the Veil

The Assumption is a sign of Divine Will to promote the value of women.

—2nd Vatican Council

And a great sign appeared in heaven:

A woman clothed with the sun,

and the moon under her feet,

and on her head a crown of twelve stars.

—Revelation 12: 1

The archetypal mother connects us to nature and to the body, connections that suggest a complex set of meanings. The female traditionally represents the cycles of nature, but her attractiveness also links her to the realm of adornment, to beautiful clothing and jewelry. The female is also the psyche, the symbol of our inner emotional life. Finally the female is the source and the maintainer of the family, both at home in the mundane tasks of daily care and in the larger sense of a civilizing, unifying force for peace in the community.

In an unforgiving climate like that of New Mexico's, the hearth and home take on inordinate power and centrality to the family, and the keeper of that flame is the female. After the male *conquistadores* and male friars had conquered the American Southwest, women arrived in the succeeding waves of immigrants, perhaps a "civilizing" series of waves. Spanish, Mexican, and Native American women all shared in this great role, which intersects with La Conquistadora's legend. Spanish society has sometimes been characterized as somewhat matriarchal, as evidenced by the practice of adding surnames to a woman's name. Some suggest that Spanish and Hispanic women have historically wielded great influence in household decisions, in contrast to more patriarchal societies.

La Conquistadora's prominence in the religious life of Santa Fe mirrors this role. While St. Francis of Assisi is the namesake of the Cathedral Basilica, veneration for either him or St. Anthony is not as widely practiced in Santa Fe. At least in outward display, La Conquistadora's reign over the faithful in Santa Fe is much more far-reaching. Her changing titles suggest how her influence has persisted over the centuries, even as circumstances have changed: Our Lady of the Assumption, then Our Lady of the Rosary, and even Our Lady-Unifier of All Peoples. The malleability has insured her survival; she has kept pace with changing times and needs of her people.

In her original title as Our Lady of the Assumption, La Conquistadora was designed so that she would appear to be gazing or inclined upwards toward heaven, with three cherubs, symbols of heavenly ascendancy, gracing her pedestal base. Church doctrine postulates that Our Lady of the Assumption was crowned in heaven to become the Queen of Heaven. Once the throne has been ascended, a queen receives a crown, cape, scepter, and other accoutrements of regal imprimatur—more elaborate garments befitting her stature and official office.

Representations of the Virgin's robes as Queen of Heaven, however, have varied in different times and cultures. La Conquistadora's original wooden robes had a mantle or veil, and Fray Angélico Chávez speculated that her garments were intricately carved, then covered in plaster, painted, and decorated with gold leaf. By the time she arrived in Santa Fe, however, she had been shorn of part of her original attire, presumably in accord with the new custom of elaborately dressing religious statues to suit various occasions. Part of the original wooden robes remained; her trunk and torso are carved to resemble a wooden dress painted gold and red. But she was intended to wear clothing, and came with a trousseau; Chávez found a receipt for a set of garments. For many years before her devotion was revitalized by Chávez and Pedro Ribera-Ortega, the oral histories reflect that the women of Santa Fe took care of La Conquistadora. After all, the intimate acts of cleaning her, dressing her, and adorning her would naturally be in the province of a woman rather than a man. In the early years, special garments and jewels may not have been easy to obtain, since supplies coming up the Camino Real may have been few and far between, and daily life must have been consumed by the need to obtain necessities and rebuild after the Pueblo Revolt. Clergy vestments and articles for the altar, perhaps cared for by women, could have found their way into garments in the same way women may have used their own cast-off dresses or fabrics until the trade expanded to include more luxurious items which could be fashioned into custom garments for her.

The act of making clothing, choosing garments, and adorning have both religious and secular significance. The act of adornment is a form of adoration, and adoration in Catholic culture is a primary act and form of veneration. Our Lady of the Assumption is not typically dressed as a simple country girl of ancient biblical times, or as a nun in a habit, or even as a young mother. Rather, she wears the garments appropriate for her role as Queen of Heaven. The act of dressing her thus engenders a focus that casts the viewer as a subject of royalty, looking upward. This approach in turn creates a chance for reflection and, for the Catholic, an opportunity for prayer.

Consuelo Hernández adorning La Conquistadora at Rosario Chapel in 1950.
Photograph by Laura Gilpin, Private Collection, Untitled, 1950, Gelatin Silver Print,
© Amon Carter Museum, Fort Worth, Texas.

The religious meaning was primary, but the secular significance of La Conquistadora's new role, a figure tended by women and dressed in garments from the community, probably contributed to the softening of her image for the public. The *conquistadores* of old, who had conquered, enslaved, and attacked New Mexico, were supplanted by an angelic presence: a symbol of unity and reconciliation, a presence who sought to win their faith and their hearts, not to enslave them. Allowing women in the community to assume responsibility for her primary care had the effect of changing La Conquistadora's role to a beneficent one, not an oppressive one. For any woman in the community, the honor of adorning and caring for La Conquistadora created a purpose outside of herself, and a purpose greater than herself. Women could be members of La Cofradía, the organization devoted to La Conquistadora, and *sacristana* (female sacristan) was the title of the woman elected to bear the responsibility of La Conquistadora's care and the preservation of her wardrobe. The sacristana organized the women of the community in the statue's care. Being part of the process that was vital to Catholicism and vital to the community's very existence was a role of great importance, given La Conquistadora's connotations as protector of the town's founders.

La Conquistadora's wardrobe soon became the major outlet for both the women's devotion and their creativity. The history of her closet mirrors the history of her origins and of her region, including an astonishing variety of pieces. Some of her robes are period costumes, emulating sixteenth and seventeenth century Spanish queens. *Colcha* embroidery in one of her capes displays the inventiveness of the maker in taming the new wools of the colony. Fray Angélico Chávez wrote of the wide variety that her garment styles have taken—everything from dresses of gingham and homespun cloth in the style of American frontier women after 1846 to the rear-bustle constricting garments of the Victorian era. During austere times, her wardrobe would fall into disrepair. Whether from poverty or prevailing fashions, her clothes sometimes matched the style of the commoner, although some contemporary pieces; Indian saris, Mandarin Chinese robes, and even a 1970s dress studded with bright green sequins worthy of a disco, hardly reflect pedestrian taste.

Women in La Cofradía made garments for La Conquistadora, but they also accepted donations, often adapting garments contributed by others. One of the oldest pieces is a cape made from a processional cope owned by Archbishop Jean Baptiste Lamy. Fray Angélico Chávez donated his military uniform to be converted into garments, replete with his chaplain's insignia, captain's stars and service ribbons. As La Conquistadora's fame grew, contributions were received from far and wide. Inuit and Eskimo residents of Holy Cross village in Alaska made a gift of an ermine-trimmed cape for her. She also has Native American jewelry and traditional Native garments from closer to home; each year during Indian Market she dons one of six traditional Native outfits, such as the pieces made for her by Dorothy Trujillo of Cochití Pueblo. Even non-Catholics design or sew garments for her; for example, Ali MacGraw commissioned an outfit from an exquisite fabric. MacGraw participated in the ceremony that surrounds the receipt of each gift: La Conquistadora is dressed in the new garments, with prayers offered on the occasion.

Gold and other rich materials feature prominently among La Conquistadora's garments. During his military duty, Chávez purchased gold cloth in Speyer, Germany, and it was used to make a cape bearing the Chávez coat-of-arms with its distinctive five keys; a small medallion on the collar underscores Chávez's connection to the penitente brotherhood of New Mexico. Former sacristana Mary Dean is especially proud of the cape she ordered in Spain during La Peregrina's 1993 trip: in Sedillo, Dean commissioned a royal blue and gold cape embroidered with gold metallic thread, requiring a year-long effort by five seamstresses. Elaborate devotional items are also part of La Conquistadora's vast inventory of possessions, such as an ornate gold cross encrusted with 200 diamonds, emeralds, and sapphires. There are also crowns that rival a monarch's, and many items of jewelry, including both elaborate historical pieces and contemporary items such as earrings or freshwater pearls. Concha Ortiz y Pino de Kleven donated a family heirloom: a necklace from 1780, given in petition for her brother-in-law's recovery from cancer. One jewel-encrusted cross was donated anonymously and sent through the mail. A child made a bracelet out of pipe cleaners and plastic beads. La Conquistadora's list of accessories includes wigs made of human hair donated by local women. Shoes, however, are not necessary; during her various restorations, La Cofradía decided to raise her garments to display the gilded cherubs at her base, which had sometimes been hidden.

Each garment is a link to history but also a petition of prayer. The sacristana receives the garment, and she may be the only other person who knows where hidden petitions or prayers are stitched into secret hiding places. This bond between the maker and the sacristana is a veiled ministry, not clandestine, but implicit and personal, not unlike, perhaps, a father confessor and his parishioner. Former sacristana Consuelo ("Connie") Hernández recalls times when small items belonging to children were sewn into the lining of La Conquistadora's garments to seek protection or intercession. The army uniforms, like Chávez's, illustrate a tradition in which veterans and their families sought La Conquistadora's intercession for a safe return from battle. All of the wedding gowns, army uniforms, and clergy vestments that have been refashioned for her, and sometimes for the Infant Jesus as well, carry stories of devotion, as do the gifts of new, custom garments. Often stories of the reasons for making these garments and wigs carry poignant tales of heart transplants, cancer operations, death and disease, but there are just as many happy stories of ordinations, births, weddings, and safe returns from wars. As Ribera-Ortega's mother said about the gown she made from a wedding dress: you pray as you sew, and the completed dress is fulfillment of a *promesa*.

The most remarkable thing about the history of adorning La Conquistadora is the way in which, perhaps because of Santa Fe's great distance from the royal closets of Europe and the dressmakers there, she became the beneficiary of the community. In the early years, there was seldom sumptuous gold cloth from Europe, and the women contributed what they had. Her caretakers gave not only of their dressmaking talents but even their own belongings, whether it was personal jewelry, sentimental trinkets, or locally-made items. She became a community work of art.

A notable instance of such art was a communal cape, a project overseen by Miguelita ("Miquelita") Hernández, who served as sacristana in the 1940s. She spread the cloak on her dining table in the family home on Old Santa Fe Trail and invited visitors "even if they couldn't sew" to contribute meaningful pieces of jewelry and filigree to be attached to the cloak. Wedding rings, earrings, family treasures, and other trinkets of the past wove a community story into the fabric, allowing many people to feel close to the figure they revered. No contribution was deemed unworthy, as a child's tiny cross hairpin suggests. Having "commoners" allowed a role in her glorification ensured her viability as a symbol, not just for the elite but for everyone, thereby ensuring her survival. The sacristana's conscious decision to democratize the process of providing for La Conquistadora by including the entire community, perhaps even non-Catholics, was an egalitarian act that wove her legend into the fabric of Santa Fe. As the community cape demonstrates, modest and anonymous gifts have been made from the entire spectrum of the community, not just from the rich and famous.

The organization that serves, protects, and venerates La Conquistadora, La Cofradía, has always had both men and women members. Such an organization will coalesce when threats by rival societies force certain groups underground to salvage core treasures, and core beliefs with them, in an "ark" of sorts against loss and destruction. In medieval Europe, the practice was often associated with guilds or other organizations devoted to maintaining special customs or practices. These organizations, however, have traditionally been mostly male—for example, the Knights Templar and the Masons. For women to have had a similar role of "saving" La Conquistadora for future generations is remarkable. Often the responsibility was passed down in a family tradition of humility and sacrifice, with generations sometimes counting both mayordomos and sacristanas in their ranks. The Hernández family, for example, may have begun its tradition of service in 1757, when Hernández ancestor Amadeo Sena served as mayordomo. Later in that same family, Miquelita Hernández served a twenty-year term as sacristana, followed by her daughter Consuelo "Connie" Hernández. But while the office may be publicly-known, the experience of caring for La Conquistadora is private: the current sacristana,

Terry García, describes the key of dressing the statue "as an act of devotion in itself." Connie Hernández, reluctant to draw personal attention to her experience, says that service brought her incredible joy, but that "Our Lady belongs to all of us, not only to one of us."

During much of La Conquistadora's history, women served her in ways other than her maintenance and clothing. In writings and archives concerning La Conquistadora, there are many references and depictions that show young women, often a quartet, carrying her in procession. Nuns and young women would have been involved in her care, and the implicit requirement of purity and chasteness would have been suitable for her devotion. Women describe their procession carrying her as not one of mere geography, traversing the few miles from the Cathedral to Rosario Chapel, but as a journey of prayer that affects them deeply. Some describe the pilgrimage as transformative, providing enlightenment, while still others process the event on physical terms, describing the sensation of tingling in the hands used to carry La Conquistadora, even days afterward.

The practice of women in procession changed, however, and now men carry La Conquistadora. Perhaps the paradigm began to shift when the convents closed and the realities of World War II drew women into the workforce in greater numbers. Sewing trinkets onto capes may have fallen to the wayside against the pragmatic needs of putting food on the table. Asking members of La Cofradía about this time period is painful, and they attribute the change to chivalric notions: that the women used to carry La Conquistadora in procession because the men formed a phalanx around her to carry weapons to protect her.

An alternative explanation might be that when La Cofradia waned, and La Conquistadora's legend was in peril, the burden of caring for her had to be spread across a bigger base; drawing men to her side ensured her survival. Both Chávez and Ribera-Ortega deliberately worked to extend her popularity and her legend. Part of the effort included the making of La Peregrina so that she could be involved in more trips and more processions, but another part involved the greater inclusion of men. Ribera-Ortega re-crafted the ceremonial *anda* or palanquin that was used to carry her in trnasport for procession. He also re-christened the newly-refurbished object as a "*paso,*" but that is more commonly akin to a large float instead of a litter. In any case, the object that formerly could be easily handled by four lithe young women became heavier and more unwieldy, requiring up to six to eight men, flanked by up to twelve more. For maneuvering steps, or if fatigued, the men occasionally rotate the burden of carrying her. Consequently, women were no longer the bearers or the honor guard, and their role has been pushed back into the closet, so to speak.

Certainly the efforts of Fray Angélico Chávez and after him, Pedro Ribera-Ortega, have contributed to a widening of La Conquistadora's appeal. Women kept the legend going originally, but the mayordomos bore the burden of financing her upkeep. Even during lean economic times, however, the mayordomos have been able to increase her 5. Mayordomo Ignacio Garcia recalled the time years ago when he worried out loud to Ribera-Ortega about fund raising concerns; Ribera-Ortega replied, "Don't worry, she always pays her bills." Both Ribera-Ortega and Chávez referenced the efforts of Aileen O'Bryan, daughter of a former state governor as a benefactor in the background, who brought money and influence to the enterprise. Chávez escorted La Peregrina to 95 remote parishes in northern New Mexico. La Conquistadora's fame grew from all these efforts, and her fame was not merely local, as may be seen by La Peregrina's many journeys. Her legend grew as word of her honor spread. In the Marian Year of 1954, Francis Cardinal Spellman of New York placed a gold crown on La Conquistadora's head in an Episcopal Coronation.

An even greater honor occurred in 1960 during Santa Fe's 350th anniversary. On June 26, a delegation from Vatican City arrived in Santa Fe for her Papal Coronation. The requirements for the Vatican to approve such an honor are high. The population of a unique geographical region must venerate the statue or artistic image for a period of 300 years. Further, a history of miraculous intercessions must have sprung up around the venerated image. In the coronation, Archbishop Egidio Vagnozzi, Apostolic Delegate to the US, Pope John XXIII's personal representative, officially sanctioned devotion to La Conquistadora and replaced her everyday crown with one constructed of gold filigree and jewels, including New Mexico turquoise. Throngs of townsfolk lined San Francisco Street to witness this rare honor, unique in the United States, with estimates of attendance ranging from 15,000 at the cathedral to 25,000 altogether, including those lining the procession route.

La Conquistadora is a study in contradictions. She has blue eyes, but other features have been described as Palestinian, with a serene gaze that speaks to many cultures and conveys emotions of tranquility and peace. What remains of her original wooden robes perhaps recall her mysterious origins—her chemise painted in the colors of the Spanish flag in deep golds and reds, accented by a delicate arabesque design reminiscent of Arabic motifs and the Holy Land. She wears a crown, carries a scepter, and has a regal wardrobe befitting a sixteenth century Spanish queen, but she is also an icon of the people who is just as comfortable in Native American garments or in humble attire. Her appeal to the faithful and the visitor alike is indisputable. Her wardrobe, a legacy of the women who cared for her, resonates with those who visit her because it embodies traces of New Mexico's past.

Her wardrobe and her collection of jewelry and religious accoutrements are striking and draw many visitors. An exact count of items has been difficult to accomplish, and current members of the Cofradía uncovered embezzlement by a former officer of some of her clothing and jewels. Her jewelry alone is valued at $200,000, but the appraisal is out-dated and is being redone. In any case, the historic value of the entire collection is priceless. The valuable pieces have been moved to a bank safety deposit box and are only rarely displayed. In 2010 two major exhibits were mounted to display approximately 100 of La Conquistadora's approximately 200 sets of garments and crown jewels. The Basilica's "Fabric of Faith" exhibit, held during Spanish Market weekend during the summer of 2010, offered a once-in-a-lifetime chance to view her most significant garments, with items placed on the altar and in the pews. This exhibit was followed by the debut of "Threads of Devotion" at the Museum of Spanish Colonial Art, run by the

Spanish Colonial Arts Society. This exhibit contained important text and historical material to augment the display of wardrobe pieces.

La Conquistadora's wardrobe has come to symbolize the great devotion of the faithful. Not only must all articles of clothing and jewelry be tracked and inventoried, but separate items for the infant Jesus—at his scant six inches in length—must be cared for as well. Garments are changed to coincide with religious holidays and special occasions, requiring meticulous care and upkeep on old garments. As Terry García notes, "We are not working with costumes for a doll; these are sacred materials worn with purpose and deep meaning." For the faithful, there is religious meaning. But even for those of other faiths or no faith, there is meaning in the stories of each item; stories of history, of culture, of devotion that in their own way are as valuable as any precious metals and jewels that La Conquistadora's closet might contain.

The smallest things can convey the greatest meaning, like the occasional feather found in La Conquistadora's chapel, left by a Native American visitor. The gentlest act can bring about the most far-reaching change, like the silk cord that replaced the customary guitar string used around La Conquistadora's neck for holding the infant Jesus. The male history of La Conquistadora starts with her origins, her travels to the New World, her journey into battle, and her return to Santa Fe. In a later chapter that male-oriented history will be continued in discussions of the cadres of clergy, the *Caballeros de Vargas* and the men of *La Cofradía*, as well as the schisms and rivalries among these groups. But the male history is not sufficient to understand La Conquistadora. She must also be viewed from the perspective of the matriarchal part of the Hispanic culture—the women who cared for her. Before male members of the *Caballeros de Vargas* and *La Cofradía* gained prominence in her care, a group of women kept vigil over La Conquistadora and enriched the culture that grew up around her.

7

The Lost Years

"Oh, what a blow that phantom gave me!" cries Cervantes's Don Quijote.

The true mystery of the world is the visible, not the invisible.

—Oscar Wilde

Although La Conquistadora has long been a symbol of cultural reconciliation in New Mexico, such reconciliation has not always come easily. La Conquistadora's popularity has ebbed and flowed, partly as a reflection of the stress of the times. In the latter half of the twentieth century, cultural and political upheavals that unsettled much of the United States affected New Mexico's delicate balance as well. As Fray Angélico Chávez noted, the expression on La Conquistadora's face reflects the sorrows of her people, and certainly there was much to be sorrowful about in the decades of the 1960s through the late 1970s.

Part of this period's story begins in earlier eras of New Mexico's history. The turmoil in the region surrounding Santa Fe, successively under the control of Spain, Mexico, and the United States created disruptive changes in political and religious organization. In 1821, when Mexican Independence caused the departure of the priests, the empty church pulpits created a void that could not be filled by diocesan priests. If the priest in the village had gone back to Mexico, the most basic and necessary religious needs of daily life and death were in limbo. In many rural or remote parts of New Mexico, the penitente brotherhood could provide these services, and, as Fray Angélico Chávez believed, acting as a human "ark" of sorts, keeping the faith alive.

Soon after Jean Baptiste Lamy came to New Mexico from France as bishop in 1851, he renewed previous campaigns to remove local influences, especially Native influences, from the church. In France, Lamy had practiced devotion to the Virgin Mary as Our Lady of Victory. Lamy failed in his attempt to introduce this title to the area, but instituted many other European practices. Local organizations like the penitentes were driven underground. Local priests were forced to impose strict tithes on the people, and charges for baptisms and other services were instituted. These measures drove a wedge between many of the local clergy and the church organization, so that rising tensions culminated in Lamy's excommunication of Padre Martínez of Taos. The rift between French clergy and local priests had repercussions for decades afterward. Some claimed, for example, that local priests were not given "tenure track" as readily as those from elsewhere and it was not until Robert Fortune Sanchez's ordination as Archbishop in 1974 that the wounds began to heal.

Lamy's campaign against local influences extended to devotional materials in the churches themselves. When he toured northern New Mexico, he destroyed *santos, retablos*, and other icons of New Mexican origin, replacing them with European images. When the railroad came to Santa Fe in the 1870s and brought more material goods from outside New Mexico, there were further changes, perhaps in part because the churches were controlled by those with an aesthetic sense developed from other places. New-fangled wallpaper arrived, and many traditional surfaces and elements were papered over. At Rosario Chapel, the altar screen that had originally been commissioned by mayordomo Antonio Jose Ortiz and other families was covered with wallpaper and the piece was ruined. False ceilings covered *vigas* and *latillas*, and American influences brought sidings and ramparts to local architecture. Interior walls at St. Francis Cathedral were covered with white paint, with Spanish Colonial altars and gold-leaf embellishments losing their place in the overall aesthetic.

In the early years of the twentieth century, interest in devotion to La Conquistadora waned. After World War II, two people were instrumental in restoring the statue to her former glory: Fray Angélico Chávez and Pedro Ribera-Ortega. Chávez's work in bringing La Peregrina to the people of northern New Mexico deserves special mention during this period.

As the 1960s began, however, the post-WWII emphasis on modernization became a major force, affecting even religious practices. The Second Vatican Council of 1962 – 1965 ("Vatican II") brought another wave of "housecleaning" to New Mexico churches, and some ancient examples of *retablos mayor* (altar screens) and murals were removed or painted plain white. Even the term "retablo" was discarded in favor of "reredos"--a non-Spanish word that did not accurately reflect the meaning of the piece known as a retablo mayor. Fray Chávez saw the church's direction as an attack on the traditions of religion in New Mexico. He criticized church hierarchy as something of a repudiation of the region's Hispanic birthright, writing a book, for example, about Padre Martínez of Taos, whom Lamy had excommunicated. Chávez's strong feelings have been traced, in part, to prejudices he experienced from his ethnicity. His research into the history of the pentitentes resonated strongly with his feelings of alienation from mainstream church culture. He believed that secret groups with local *moradas* could preserve faith, tradition, and Hispanic culture against French, American, and other outside influences. In 1971, Chávez left the Franciscan Order. Father Jack Clark Robinson, O.F.M., PhD, says that when Chávez left, he was given an opportunity to leave within church law but refused to sign the requisite paperwork. He simply drove away from the friary, leaving a note on the chalkboard with instructions on how the car could be retrieved.

In Santa Fe, the post-war's modernization also increasingly meant commercialization and more tourism. Tourism especially affected the Fiesta de Santa Fe, the annual celebration of the city's reconquest, in which

La Conquistadora had always played a major role. The Fiesta had been promoted heavily by the Chamber of Commerce, and crowds grew, even including fraternity boys bused to town from Albuquerque. The event lost its quality as a family and community celebration, and residents feared for their safety after a fatality on the Plaza. The near-bacchanalia quality of the annual burning of Zozobra threatened to overshadow the event's historic and religious underpinnings. In 1963, St. Francis Cathedral withdrew its support of Fiesta de Santa Fe.

The late 1960s and 1970s saw the nation as a whole grow more unsettled as the tumultuous civil rights movement spread from one group to another, the Vietnam War undermined respect for authority, and the baby boomers reached their teens. The backdrop of the Watergate scandal and the civil rights movement seemed to overshadow the perilous world of a small religious icon tucked away in her chapel wall. In New Mexico, the spirit of the civil rights movement came together with local tensions reaching back to the region's early period to create a battleground on the issue of land grants. The Spanish crown's system of land grants had a long history in New Mexican culture, creating a class system of sorts between the descendants of the founding families and those who had immigrated more recently. If your family had been given land by the Spanish crown, it meant you became a *Hidalgo*—a nobleman or a "someone" of title. Growing tensions came to a head in 1967 when a land grant movement headed by Reies Lopez Tijerina, Chicano activist with connections to *La Raza Unida*, the immigrant farm workers activist group, turned militant. A raid on the Rio Arriba courthouse at Tierra Amarilla in northern New Mexico produced a gun battle. Centuries-old history and recent social upheavals had caused an event that shocked the state to its core.

During this period, society was being fractured, and the old affiliations often went by the wayside. Instead of belonging to organizations in a profession, a community, or a church, people might join organizations furthering political or social causes, or causes celebrating ethnic groups. The growing tendency to question authority meant that many people were less interested in organized religion, so that the number of Catholics began to decline. Women's roles changed, and the echo of the women's movement slowly spread into cloistered fronts, reaching into the church where women, who had historically stayed obedient and silent, suddenly found their collective voice. The number of initiates joining the priesthood or serving as nuns declined dramatically. Convents closed and one theme of the women's movement that denigrated "women's work" might have factored into a perceived decline in the care and maintenance of La Conquistadora. Times were changing rapidly in many ways. While the changes were certainly not all harmful, those who were devoted to traditions found these changes difficult.

For those who were devoted to La Conquistadora, the low point in those tense years occurred in 1973. On March 19, 1973, following a two-year string of thefts from churches and penitente *moradas*, La Conquistadora was stolen from the cathedral and held for ransom. The entire city seemed traumatized by the theft, with newspaper commentators and Governor Bruce King describing her as the "patron saint of New Mexico." Her kidnappers hid her in a mineshaft and demanded a ransom of $150,000. With the ransom note came a small cross that they had pried from La Conquistadora's crown. After many tense days, and as her reward fund grew by donations from the Caballeros de Vargas and the Fiesta Council, the police traced a call received at the cathedral to a 17-year-old boy. He led the police to a mine in the Manzano Mountains, and her recovery was announced on April 15. When La Conquistadora was recovered, she was missing her crown, but it was later found buried in an arroyo near St. John's College. Many other missing items were found buried out in Arroyo Hondo. An 18-year-old boy had also been involved in the multiple thefts.

Ribera-Ortega, who was mayordomo at the time of La Conquistadora's theft, was traumatized by the ordeal. His writings go into great detail about his day-to-day worries about the theft: "I worked with policemen Paul Baca and Mike Montoya and one day a strange letter arrived in the mail addressed to me, and written in Italian! Her little cross off the crown was in the letter." Later, he received an anonymous postcard [with a picture] of the cathedral and a message about a package with dimensions of 12 inches by 42 inches, implying her size. When La Conquistadora was recovered, his descriptions were often overly dramatic—for example, saying that when she was found she was surrounded by dynamite, or that she allowed herself to be stolen to revitalize the veneration of her image and to recover the many other missing items, and, lastly, that court officials had ordered that she be kept "in jail" (implying that she was behind bars) until adequate plans for her security could be made. But Ribera-Ortega's concern was not misplaced. Upon her return, he described her head as scratched and her condition as forlorn and dirty. She was all in one piece, however, so he took her to the cloistered Discalced Carmelite Nuns for a clean *manta* and raiment. Later, he asked the two police officers who helped rescue her to serve as honor guards for her triumphant return procession from the courthouse to the cathedral. Ribera-Ortega found great comfort in the safe return of two Vietnam War veterans to Santa Fe on April 28, two weeks after La Conquistadora's safe return; the public mood also seemed to be lifted.

The decades of the 1960s and 1970s were not entirely years of gloom, however. The nation's first Hispanic Bishop, Roberto Fortune Sánchez, was appointed Archbishop of the Santa Fe Diocese in 1974. Sanchez reintroduced the Christmas *posadas* tradition that had been lost and reinvigorated the celebration of Hispanic culture. The civil rights movement may have contributed to growing interest in local artistic and cultural traditions during this period. In 1975 the *retablos mayor* (also known as "reredos") at Rosario Chapel, originally commissioned by don Antonio José y Ortiz, was restored. It bears the Spanish tribute to its creator and patron as follows: *"fresquis reredos pintada por [don] Pedro Antonio Fresquís en 1809, restauracion hecha en 1975 por la Cofradía de la Conquistadora con fondos del Monismer trust."*

By the 1980s, La Cofradía, which Archbishop Byrne had reauthorized in 1956, decided to find a *santero* and commissioned an altarpiece fitting for La Conquistadora at Rosario Chapel. Unlike other examples of the *retablos mayor* that usually have images of many of the saints, a special *nicho* for Our Lady was built and also a separate place for a *retablo* of San José Bandito. At the Cathedral, Artist Robert Cary was part of the restoration work to erase the effects of Vatican II. He worked on two fragments of the ancient *parróquia* altarpiece, the permanent retablos mayor at the La Conquistadora shrine. A third section was added to complete the retablos mayor. Underneath four layers of regular household white paint was the original 1714 gilded altarpiece, but when the paint was scraped away, the original gold leaf was ruined. Cary started over and in six weeks finished a newly gilded altarpiece that Archbishop Byrne blessed. Fray Angélico Chávez, who had reconciled himself somewhat to the church, aided in the design of the new altar screens for La Conquistadora Chapel, as he had hand-painted the photograph of Our Lady of Light altar screen from *La Castrense*, Santa Fe's military chapel (which Lamy had sold) now installed at Cristo Rey Church.

Thus the church celebrated a return to its traditional arts for decoration and devotion. Archbishop's Sánchez's efforts to restore *las posadas* tradition at Christmas was only one part of a general growth in the celebration of Hispanic culture. For example, families that had "anglicized" their names, or who had dropped the custom of adding surnames in strings (Ortiz y Pino to Pino) began to revert to the traditional custom. Prominence in use of Hispanic names began to recur, and even the Cathedral reflected the flowering multiculturalism by installing artwork by Spanish and Native artists, such as the imposing figure on the front terrace of Blessed Kateri Tekakwitha by Native American sculptor Estella C. Loretto. As in the classic jewelry designs combining silver mined by the Spanish and turquoise discovered by the Native Americans, the merging currents of Southwestern culture made for a potent aesthetic.

Two events in 1992 close out this tumultuous period. The first was tragic and perhaps reflected the turmoil that the era had produced; the second looked forward to a truer reconciliation of cultures. In August of 1992, Rev. Reynaldo Rivera, the rector of St. Francis Cathedral, was slain at the hands of an unknown assailant after responding to a telephone call asking for a priest to administer last rites. Rivera's body, with a gunshot wound to the abdomen, was found in the dirt near the ghost town of Waldo, south of Santa Fe. His death, however, created a great outpouring of concern. Three hundred priests came to the cathedral, and thousands of people lined the streets to honor him.

The second event in 1992 saw an historic ceremony that moved the city's cultural reconciliation forward. Archbishop Roberto F. Sánchez initiated a new parish in Santa Fe called *Nuestra Señora de la Paz* to honor *Nuestra Señora del Rosario, La Conquistadora.* In recognition once again of her shift to meet the needs of her people and the times, her title was amended to La Conquistadora, Queen of Peace, Our Lady of Peace, *Nuestra Señora de la Paz.* This was a fundamental change in how La Conquistadora related to her community, as it had both religious significance and socio-political significance as a form of symbolic reconciliation between Hispanics and Native Americans. In the context of residual tensions from the Vietnam War, the implicit call for peace in her name stood as a radical shift in the church's traditional neutral stance. Her name title was translated as "unifier of faith" and deliberately dropped any reference to conquest or dominance of one culture over another.

So a new era began: La Conquistadora's countenance could reflect new hope of a revitalized church, relevant to its parish and to all the people of the city. The church and the Fiesta grew back together.

Much has been written of the theme of Christianity as a tool of social domination or "civilization" and Columbus's interpretation of what he saw in the New World when he wrote that native populations regarded him as a man from heaven, to be showered with gifts. In contrast, little is known of the legends of those who were conquered; probably they would not corroborate Columbus's Euro-centric view. In New Mexico, however, the Native population has not been obliterated and destroyed as it was in many other places in the Americas; rather, Native people continued their culture even as they took part in the broadening community. In New Mexico, the invading culture itself was in a sense conquered. The Native populations lent their culture to the Spanish, and we have witnessed a unique blending of the two, with artist/historians such as Charlie Carrillo describing the Hispanics as being "pueblo-cized" and blended in their cultures, architecture, cuisine, artwork, and more. These two intertwining branches preserved the indigenous people, who grafted Catholicism onto their own beliefs, so that today it is not uncommon to find both the native *kiva* and the Catholic chapel co-existing in a Pueblo, and healing spots once "pagan" in ownership, selected as the place to erect a Catholic church. The situation in New Mexico is similar to Spain's history as a blending of cultures due in part to its geographical proximity to both northern European peoples and the Moors from northern Africa. The waves of Spanish people that spread throughout the world, including the incursion into the Aztec and Mexican tribal peoples, have led some to term the Spanish people as the one true "cosmic" race, a blend of the three main peoples on Earth. The "lost years" served to reunite New Mexicans—already a lost tribe in Fray Angélico Chávez's estimation—with their traditional heritage.

Other kinds of cultural reconciliations have taken place in recent years as well. When the Cathedral of Santa Fe withdrew from the Fiesta in 1963, the reasons were tourism and commercialism. Since that time tourism has only increased. Perhaps, however, Santa Fe has gained experience in allowing tourism and the life of the city to coexist. Santa Fe also has transcended the confines of mere geography to become a "brand" connoting many values and images, a brand flexible enough to sell perfume, cookies, automobiles and all sorts of commercial products to the marketplace. Such commercialism is a source of frustration to many who live in the city, but it in fact speaks of the city's beauty, the complex set of values it represents, and its status as an icon of the mix of cultures, much like La Conquistadora herself. The "new age" mystique that the city bears is another instance of cultural reconciliation, as people come to the region, discover its natural power, hear the echoes of distant realms and times, and leave their old selves behind.

We shouldn't omit one more result of the "lost years." In his Cofradía journals, Pedro Ribera-Ortega made a small but profound change to the vernacular by beginning to reference La Cofradía as a brotherhood *and* a sisterhood, reflecting, perhaps, that the social turmoil of the women's movement had reached behind the protective walls of the church and shifted the paradigm.

La Conquistadora in Native American dress at Rosario Chapel, June 2008.
Photograph by Carolee J. Friday.

8

The Sword and the Shield

The thorn and the flesh belong together.

—Oskar Loerke

Remain faithful until death and I will give you the crown of life.

—Revelation 2:10

If the women of the community furnish and tend to the veil and "soft goods" for the queen, it is the male half of the community that forms the hard shield between her and peril. While an earlier chapter told the story of the women who cared for La Conquistadora over the years, this section focuses on how, with the leadership of Fray Angélico Chávez and Pedro Ribera-Ortega, the organization known as La Cofradía restored men's involvement in La Conquistadora's protection and the preservation of her traditions. These two men, both childless bachelors, have contributed the most to the discovery of La Conquistadora's history and to the growth of her legend. Fray Angélico Chávez was born in 1910 and ordained as a Franciscan priest in 1937. Ribera-Ortega, born in 1931, though he displayed talent for liturgy, but did not follow him into the priesthood; instead, he became a teacher. Both men were members of La Cofradía, the organization devoted to La Conquistadora, and both spent their lives in service to her and to the traditions that she represents.

Both men belonged to the *pentitente* groups known collectively as *La Hermandad*, a parallel brotherhood of the Confraternity that was extremely secretive and more radical vis-à-vis the formal church hierarchy. Fray Angélico Chávez saw the church hierarchy as not always worthy of preservation. He felt that the tradition of Catholicism among the Spanish settlers in New Mexico had been abrogated by Vatican II, Lamy, the civil rights movement, and the suppression of local priests, and he must have considered his pentitente forbearers along with La Conquistadora, as part of a faith which had to be saved at all costs.

Chávez devoted many years to the study of La Conquistadora's past. His two books, *Our Lady of Conquest* (1948) and *La Conquistadora/The Autobiography of an Ancient Statue* (1954) were milestones in recovering her history. Chávez based his research on a variety of records from New Mexico, Mexico, and Spain. The earliest New Mexico document dates from 1680, probably because earlier material was lost in the Pueblo Revolt. Chávez's work tells the history of La Conquistadora, but also of La Cofradía, the organization devoted to her protection and care. The story begins in 1626, when Friar Alonso de Benavídes brought the statue to Santa Fe Benavídes is credited with initiating the service organization for *Nuestra Señora de la Asuncíon*, as she was known at that time. La Cofradía probably remained associated with the clergy during its early years. By the 1650s the *Cofradia del Rosario* (confraternity of the Rosary) as it was originally called, had adopted the Our Lady of the Rosary statue as the image of the patroness of the group. By the time of the Pueblo Revolt, she was already being referred to as La Conquistadora, so the confraternity's name changed as well. Chávez found a 1661 record in Spain of the group's existence, and also notes a later 1692 reference that points to the group's efforts before the Pueblo Revolt and suggests the link to the organized church: "A Silver lamp which was brought out of New Mexico and which was kept at the Convent of Socorro and was returned to the Confraternity because it was its property. Furthermore, a silver diadem which belonged to the convent of El Paso and was exchanged for a silver crown that belonged to this confraternity."[4]

After the Pueblo Revolt, La Conquistadora was removed from Santa Fe and taken into exile with soldiers and settlers near the current city of El Paso. Documentation belonging to that period is also scarce, but Chávez painstakingly unraveled some early history from fragmentary material. In an inventory fragment, a statement by Captain Alonso Del Río, mayordomo, said he received all of the Cofradía property from Francisco Gómez Robledo, who was mayordomo in 1684. He noted that the organization was in arrears, perhaps due to the long period of exile and the harsh conditions in El Paso, where settlers lived in constant peril from attacks by Manso Indians. This captain's log hints at the church's oversight.

On the reverse side of the inventory sheets was a record of an Official Visitation, a review of sorts by Father Pedro Gómez, Vice Custos and Ecclesiastical Judge on October 18, 1688. Gómez found "some articles old and outworn, and regulates the disposal of them; then in his handwriting he makes a complete inventory of the images, clothing, and jewels."

Ribera-Ortega has suggested that La Conquistadora's fragile existence created a cause for the exiled settlers to unite behind, coalescing around an ideal instead of material possessions as they struggled for survival. Thus the period of exile and reconquest is perhaps the time in which La Cofradía was becoming somewhat autonomous, though still with strong ties to the church. Certainly de Vargas was devoted to La Conquistadora, as his journals mention, and was a member of the organization. Chávez notes that de Vargas donated costly items to La Cofradía and was later elected mayordomo. In 1712, eight years after de Vargas's death, a proclamation was signed to establish an annual commemoration of the reconquest, in La Conquistadora's honor. Perhaps beginning with de Vargas's governorship, La Cofradía was also associated with those who held secular power. De Vargas's right-hand man, don Juan Páez Hurtado, began as a simple soldier under de Vargas's command, but grew in power and influence. He was elected to La

Cofradía, served as mayordomo, and eventually became governor, serving in 1704 and 1705.

La Cofradía continued to be active in New Mexico throughout the 1700s. The inventory fragments that Chávez found, continuing to the year 1714, are filled with references to additional gifts by individual devotees of Our Lady, visits by various *Padres Custodios*, and receipts of books and property by incoming mayordomos. In 1714, members of La Cofradia began building the adobe chapel. When the cathedral was rebuilt in the 1860s, the chapel was preserved inside the imposing basilica of sandstone. Rosario Chapel, situated as it is in a cemetery, became an ancestral visiting place for memories of the dead generations buried there. Pedro Ribera-Ortega contributed research about La Cofradía during the 1700s. He described the turmoil in the region during that era, when the Candelario Report to the viceroy stated that "the people of New Mexico were in dire straits from continuous attacks made against them by their barbarous enemies in the wild Apaches, Comanches, and Navajos . . . he inhabitants elected a special new heavenly patron to intercede for them before the Divine Majesty . . . a Conquistadora."

Chávez and Ribera-Ortega contributed to both the history and the legend of La Conquistadora and La Cofradía, linking them to a long history of organizations devoted to the Virgin Mary. Ribera-Ortega, for example, wrote of how October, the Month of the Holy Rosary, with its feast day on the seventh known as *la Fiesta de la Virgen del Santo Rosario,* had its origins in the Battle of Lepanto in 1571 under Pope Pius V. Both men were tireless in their research and in their devotion. Chávez became an oracle of sorts, "speaking" for La Conquistadora, while Ribera-Ortega functioned more as a town crier, spreading the word wherever he could. Both thus continued the tradition of "troubadours of Our Lady," poets who had blended history and legend in innocent abandon to celebrate not tales of the Knights of the Round Table trying to win a fair lady's hand, but instead the stories of crusaders whose purpose was to exalt the heavenly Blessed Mother and to promote the faith.

After Chávez and Ribera-Ortega had laid the historical foundations for La Cofradía's early existence and encouraged others to join them in devotion, the church did more to acknowledge the group. The publication of Chávez's 1948 book probably contributed to the organization's growth in numbers and to its official recognition. The church hierarchy often blesses movements only after they have been set in motion by dedicated leaders and then gained popular legitimacy.

At any rate, in 1956, under the direction of Archbishop Edwin Vincent Byrne, the 300 year old Confraternity of La Conquistadora, La Cofradía, which had lapsed during the nineteenth century, was revitalized. The *Caballeros de Vargas* were founded in June of 1956 and were made the official honor guard of La Conquistadora in 1957, but historic antecedents for the group dated back to don Diego de Vargas's era.

The revitalized organization kept much of the structure of the original Cofradía, whose membership had been limited to those of Spanish descent. The organization, formally known as *La Cofradía de María Santísima,* was headed by the *Mayordomo,* or president. The *Secretario* (secretary), recorded memberships and made announcements of devotional events. The *Sacristana,* or wardrobe mistress and caregiver, kept Our Lady's image and altar-shrine in order and cleanliness, inventoried devotional gifts and their origins, and arranged for flowers and candles. The *Tesorero* (treasurer) collected *cuotas* (annual dues) in kind and currency. Accountings reflect that in the original organization, very little in currency was collected, and items of many kinds are noted. Early tesoreros traveled throughout New Mexico to collect dues, often in sheep.

Chávez and Ribera-Ortega held varying posts within La Cofradía and the *Caballeros de Vargas,* sometimes simultaneously and other times sequentially. With Chávez being from the clergy-class and Ribera-Ortega on the "outside," they sometimes had interlocking dual and triple roles, serving as mayordomos of La Cofradía, honor guard members, and chief proponents of La Conquistadora's publicity and press relations. La Cofradía and the *Caballeros de Vargas,* also interacted with local civic organizations such as the Fiesta Council, and their influence stretched to elements of city and state government as well. Such links between devotional groups, civic organizations, and government date back to the days of de Vargas and his protégé Hurtado. This process has been repeated throughout New Mexico history; the knitting of secular and religious ties is so close that the church works its ways deep into the government of New Mexico.

Around the central figures of Chávez and Ribera-Ortega a great tradition of service grew, alongside the twin tradition of devotion to La Conquistadora's image that made Santa Fe into a place known for a special connection to the holy, the mysterious, and the divine. But with the daily exercise of power, internecine quarrels and rivalries have at times driven deep divisions into the community. The fact that such struggles are rarely reported may be due to the organization's policy of secrecy. La Cofradía considers itself not only an organization for the administration of La Conquistadora's protection and care, but also, in the worst of times, as an ark against the loss of valuable traditions. Ribera-Ortega made much of the fact no specific references or mentions were made in contemporary outside sources of the existence of the original confraternity and its activities, so it follows that there should be no outright reference to the organizational struggles that continually occur. Something within the internal structure of the confraternity could be triggered in times of peril to activate the steps necessary to take La Conquistadora to safety or to hide her guards from sight. As with the Knights Templar and the penitentes, an organization that existed at least marginally on the surface of society could at any time be driven underground to save itself.

Some of the secrecy of this "off the books" operation has been diminished in modern times by the fact that La Cofradía does not operate without the oversight of the church. Key positions in La Cofradía, such as sacristana do not have an official counterpart in church hierarchy, but there is a parallel position of church sacristan. While the sacristan does not change the statue's clothing, this parallelism between the two organizations underscores the way in which the church organization shadows its own shadow. With La Cofradía's manpower ability, a funding structure, and a mission statement, it appears autonomous, seemingly apart from the church or "of the people" while the church can maintain discreet oversight at a distance.

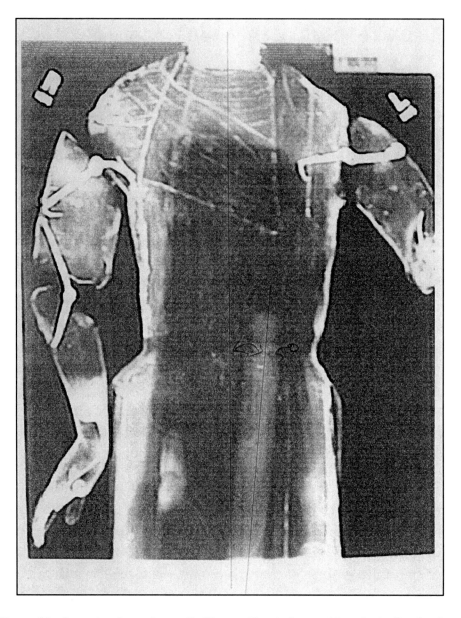

X-ray of La Conquistadora taken at St. Vincent Hospital, 1997. Note the inclined pole or standard, at an angle approximately ten degrees to the vertical plane of the statue.

In an organic fashion then, La Cofradía, like La Conquistadora herself, not only changed over time but, due to the efforts of Chávez and Ribera-Ortega, began to thrive again. Don Diego de Vargas did not live to see the shrine he had promised to La Conquistadora. Even after it was built in 1714, there were long periods when the maintenance of her shrine and of other traditional structures may have faltered in honoring the beautiful and traditional arts and modes of devotion. Notwithstanding Chávez's and Ribera-Ortega's support and even physical toil in the restoration of de Vargas's chapel and the La Conquistadora Chapel, their greatest achievements lie in their research, their writings, their popularization, and their unceasing devotion to La Conquistadora and the cultural traditions that she represents. In essence they saved a culture from destruction. This is the tradition La Cofradía carries forward today.

We can see the men who bore this tradition almost as part of a modern knighthood. The tradition of knighthood and chivalry was born in the necessity to take up arms to defend the crown and the faith. The legend of Santa Fe as a royal city and its status as a city of faith may in some sense link back to an order of knights. In recent times, some female elements of the La Cofradía's history have been lost; originally, women carried La Conquistadora in procession. With Ribera-Ortega's re-design of the magnificent *anda* or palanquin made to carry her in procession, so heavy that women could no longer carry her, the maternal quiet surrounding her has perhaps gone. In its place has come the rise of fraternal organizations known popularly for members wearing authentic seventeenth century costume to represent don Diego de Vargas and his staff. Women still play an important part, however, and the tradition of nobility and service still lives on, for both women and men.

La Cofradía may have had a tumultuous past, but the organization has survived exile and political rivalries. In the period after the Pueblo Revolt, according to Ribera-Ortega, La Conquistadora motivated settlers to continue their struggles, and her influence can be seen as coloring New Mexico's daily life and history. Ribera-Ortega suggested that the confraternity in its best sense is truly a devotional organization, voluntary and associational with no need for by-laws or written documents, since an act of devotion is subjective and personal. But a sense of "belonging" helped Ribera-Ortega to surmise that her primary sources of membership drew from two main categories: the very affluent and the very poor. Documents and rules did grow up around the group's activities, but were not imposed rigidly; rather, united as devotees, what they had in common crossed the entire spectrum of the community and helped Santa Fe to achieve renown as an egalitarian town.

Ribera-Ortega ascribed the organizations' ascendancy to its sole purpose was to honor La Conquistadora with zealous affection. He asserted that there was nothing mundane about this role, and that because devotion to her was solely spiritual, the only routine aspect of her care was making an inventory of material offerings necessary to observe her feast and to keep her in a state befitting Her Marian Majesty and to assure the prayers and suffrages in her name for the living and deceased members of La Cofradia. As a last step in making devotion the true basis of honoring La Conquistadora through her confraternity, Ribera-Ortega encouraged anyone in the community to join. Dues for this first "public" offering outside cathedral confines began at $2.00. No qualifications were necessary to belong except great devotion and love for Christ's mother.

In his book *Symbol and Conquest*, author Ronald L. Grimes analyzed how the annual Fiesta celebration in Santa Fe has changed since its inception, and he noted that the queen's importance grew steadily since the early 1970s. "Regardless of the style and scope of the public drama, it has consistently envisioned or proclaimed the end of cultural conflict, even while enacting it."[5] Many of the schisms in our society have their roots in La Conquistadora's earliest days and have played out through the centuries through various social and political movements in which she has sometimes played a part. She holds two references for society, as mother and conqueror, and we have seen that this dual nature allows her fluidity as a symbol to continue her prevailing presence in Santa Fe's spiritual and cultural existence.

Originally enthroned at Rosario Chapel, her permanent home is now the La Conquistadora Chapel at the Cathedral Basilica of St. Francis of Assisi, and although she now only leaves the Basilica twice each year in processional journeys, her appearance is the stuff of legend and makes her the star of countless dramas in the pageant that is Santa Fe.

9

In Between Us

For we are all strangers before thee,

and sojourners, as were all our fathers:

our days on the earth are as a shadow,

and there is none abiding.

—I Chronicles 29:15

And to the woman were given two wings of a great eagle;

that she might fly into the wilderness,

into her place,

where she is nourished for a time . . . from the face of the serpent.

—Revelation 12:14

In the art of Japanese flower arrangement, spaces between objects are emphasized, and the intervals of emptiness can form a pattern that highlights the interface between positive and negative. The history of La Conquistadora has been much like that pattern: times of great stress and sorrow interspersed with great glory and goodness. There are so many different types and kinds of stories that her power as an eternal symbol contains delicate gradations, the chiaroscuro between dark and light, an aura, a crepuscular cloud, broken by rays of gold.

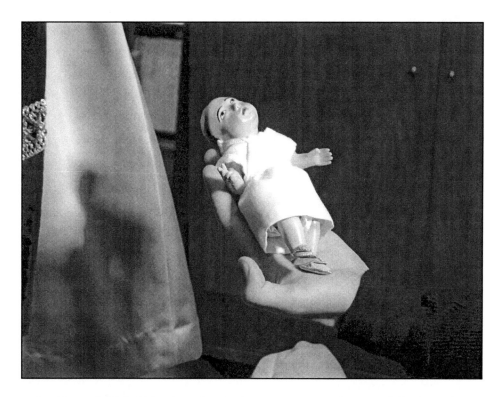

The Christ Child, held by Terry García, Sacristana, 2009. Photograph by the author.

This fluidity in her meaning is in contrast to the hard edge of the Christian cross. The symbol of the cross stands for the simultaneity of death and resurrection; it is a definite message at once specific to Christ and general to all believers. With La Conquistadora, her archetypal character as a true symbol cannot be confused with allegory. In other words, she is not merely an example of a discrete moment in time or a universal mother, but has more power as the Inscrutable, with depth and multiple meanings, yet a core of meaning that unites her many themes.

Her serene countenance is in stark contrast to most representations of the crucified Jesus in the Southwestern iconography: a bloodied, beaten depiction of extreme suffering and pain. Much has been written about how this Jesus resonated with the Spanish incursion; those who had suffered to escape persecution in Spain, or to get to the New World, or even those who had themselves suffered at the hands of the conquerors could identify with Jesus on the Cross. Comparisons have been made to the more Anglo custom of venerating the resurrected Christ, beaming with heavenly cherubs from his ascent in the golden clouds. La Conquistadora is neither or she is perhaps a fusion of the two. Her face bears signs of her suffering, but her overall demeanor shows that she will prevail.

This key attribute makes her value as a symbol cut across many cultures and peoples, allowing all individuals access to her inner meaning; as T.S. Eliot said "the suggestiveness of the aura around a bright clear centre, that you cannot have the aura alone." The concept of syncretism suggests that the religious cannot be separated from the secular, as evidenced by the prevalence of household shrines in Santa Fe's popular culture, or her making an appearance in the kitchen or on the windowsill, in the many miniature iterations of her. These appearances in many parts of life are in accordance with Santa Fe as a concept, with its memories of different peoples, and with its "mood of landscape" as Fray Angélico Chávez would say. That landscape evokes other-wordly connections, with La Conquistadora a link between what is here and what is out there. To trace her lineage back to Spain is to trace her back to the stars. She came from beyond.

She became a fused metaphor, a synthesis of several gradations of meaning molded into one commanding image. She is the expression of a complex idea; layered, not by analytical or objective measures, but by the startling clarity with which she has been perceived in relation to her subjects. While few legendary miracles have been attributed to her, the smallest miracle of her continued existence and vitality as a symbol has, perhaps, even more power. Our Lady of Guadalupe, described by church officials as national to Mexico but also supra-national in Latin America, may have greater significance on a worldwide scale. If La Conquistadora is merely statewide or regional in scope, she may not rank as high in renown in the pantheon of Mary figures around the world, but her nature has worked its way into the New Mexican culture in a profound sense.

She came to this area as an alien of sorts, almost a talisman against darkness. Aliens that succeed do so by adopting local customs; her trait of self adaptation makes her unique and not a stranger to the people. Like Alexander the Great, the Macedonians, and Viking warriors, her success can be traced to the blank slate, absorbing what she conquered and marrying herself to the people so that their traditions grew up around her and modified her meaning.

While she did not invade the New World and instantaneously "convert" herself to its people, the fact that she could adopt some of the nature and characteristics of the "place" she inhabited meant that she could meet more of the challenges of "residing" here. Her many physical journeys in the outer world are matched by the spiritual journeys of the inner world.

Sharks have a seventh sense, the ability to detect the presence of electromagnetic charges around them emanating from other creatures, so even if their vision, smell, or touch cannot operate, they can still connect to the external world. The magic of La Conquistadora is not unlike this preternatural ability; she is connected to her people by the people around her, and the dynamic of drawing information from them, for them, and about them, gives her the ability to move through the public subconscious at will.

That she can coexist between worlds places her spatially between "us" as the people in her royal seat. In a purely physical sense, she inhabits a geography of Santa Fe and of New Mexico, but she also inhabits spiritually the Catholic "Mother Church" in the region of the Southwest; visitors take her "home" with them throughout the world as well. And in terms of cults or non-affiliated groups of believers, she rules the hearts of those devoted to her image, making her both a royal queen and a common queen. This is how she both mediates and transcends time and space. For immigrants to Santa Fe, she is a symbol of the journey. For those with a dark past, she is a symbol of new beginnings and redemption. For those grieving, she is a symbol of comfort. This quality of "in between-ness" gives her iconography a reference point for everyone.

While she is true to her religion, she has also seen it fit to be true to man, or to her people. Fray Angélico Chávez left his Franciscan Order at one point, but he was never completely stripped of his identity as a priest. Similarly, La Conquistadora can traffic in the secular world, drifting into city-wide celebrations, "apparating," if you will, into the popular consciousness, and seeming to be part of the smaller dramas—weddings, funerals, tourist visits to the Basilica—of the city, so that her image becomes identified with particular values that are secular and religious at once. This ability to operate on numerous planes of existence at the same time makes her eternally powerful.

Afterword

All truths lie waiting in all things.

They unfold themselves more fragrant than . . . roses from living buds,

whenever you fetch the spring sunshine moistened with summer rain.

But it must be in your self. It shall come from your soul. It shall be love.

—Walt Whitman

And first, he was faultless in his five senses,

Nor found ever to fail in his five fingers,

And all his fealty was fixed upon the five wounds

That Christ got on the cross, as the creed tells;

And wherever this man in melee took part,

His one thought was of this, past all things else,

That all his force was founded on the five joys

That the high Queen of heaven had in her child.

And therefore, as I find, he fittingly had

On the inner part of his shield her image portrayed,

That when his look on it lighted, he never lost heart.

The fifth of the five fives followed by this knight . . . .

—Unknown, "Sir Gawain and the Green Knight"

La Conquistadora has seldom been taken down from her niche in her chapel except for changing her garments and her annual processions to Rosario Chapel in June and at Fiesta in September. However, when Fray Angélico Chávez died in 1996, she was taken down from her ledge and allowed to preside near his coffin where the great *padre* lay in state for the rosary.

She was attired in the Chávez *traje* made of gold cloth and the Chávez *escudo de armas* (coat-of-arms). Pedro Ribera-Ortega, the padre's former altar boy had, as *mayordomo,* the privilege of being part of his honor guard during the traditional *velorio.*

The eulogies of sorrow know no end; we feel his loss still. The great chronicler of our past could sing of his people no more; who will sing for the troubadour? The songs of love and chivalry are ephemera and with his death are gone, but the message endures. As the poet Jimmy Santiago Baca has said in describing Chávez's effect on his people: he was like the sunlight that cannot choose what to nourish, its light shines on everything, without bias, and his gifts are endless.

Like the five keys on the Chávez coat of arms, we are left with five clues to the eternal mysteries: the first key is the entrance into the unknown, the second key invites adventure, the third key promises a secret rendezvous, the fourth key symbolizes a secret kept and the last key, the most important of all, reveals the desire for God.

Fray Angélico Chávez with La Conquistadora.
Photograph by Laura Gilpin, Museum of New Mexico Collection,
DCA Neg. No. 9839. 1950, Gelatin Silver Print,
© Amon Carter Museum, Fort Worth, Texas.

Mayordomos and Sacristanas (Modern)

At press time, *La Cofradía de la Conquistadora* is compiling a comprehensive list of Mayordomos and Sacristanas; the list below may contain errors or omissions. Church archives reflect that church officials had differences of opinion on how and where to record accent marks in Spanish names, and sometimes, as Pedro Ribera-Ortega's writings reflect, his exhaustion gave the accent mark the power to levitate—moving to new locations, to strange places where it had never gone before. Accordingly, I apologize in advance for any errors or omission in these lists.

Mayordomos

Francisco Gómez Robledo 1656–1659

Francisco Gómez Robledo 1664

Franciso Gómez Robledo 1684

Alonso de Rio 1685–1691

Francsico de Anaya Almazon 1691

Alonso Cristóbal de Tapia 1692

Don Diego de Vargas 1692–1693

Don Diego de Vargas 1704

Juan Paéz Hurtado 1704

Bernardino de Sena 1717–1765

Amadeo Sena 1757

Tomás Antonion Sena 1765

Don Carlos 1771

Don Barolomé Fernández 1771

Don Antonio José Ortiz 1772

Don Blas García 1773

Don Francisco Têbol Navarro 1773

Don Diego Antonio Baca 1773

Don Toribio Ortiz 1774

Don Manuel Sáez de Garvisu 1774

Don Juan Antonio Ortiz 1775

Don Juan Galves 1775

Tomás Sena 1776

Don Antonio José Ortiz 1776–1806

Don Juan Antonio Ortiz (second term) 1778
(offered his services as perpetual mayordomo)

Don Cristóbal Vigil

Antonio Ortiz

Tony Blea

Medardo Ortiz

Frank Santana

Téofilo Rivera

David Ortiz

Fred Garcia

Juan B. Valdés 1956

Pedro Ribera-Ortega, 1985–2003

Ignacio Garcia, 2003–

Sacristanas (Modern)

Doña Miguelita ("Miquelita") Sena de Hernández 1956–1970
 (mother of Consuelo Hernández)

Lottie C. LeBow

Helen Romero, served two terms in the 1970s

Estefanita Martinez

Consuelo Hernández, served two terms

Becky Archuleta

Celia Medrano

Mary Dean, served two terms

Emelda Martinez, served two terms, 2001 through 2005

Terry García, June 2005–

Prayer to Our Lady
In Her Title of La Conquistadora

O Lady of Conquering Love, promised in Eden as the Woman whose Seed would crush the Serpent's Head, help us to conquer evil in our midst and in our hearts with the grace of your Son, Jesus Christ, Our God and Our Savior!

Our Lady of Conquering Love, through your motherhood of Our Savior, who is True God and True Man, help us to overcome all errors regarding His Person and the Church that He founded for His Glory and our salvation!

O Lady of conquering Love, through Jesus, who is the Prince of Peace and our Universal King, convert by his Divine Power, which is above all human might, the infidels and all the enemies of His Peace!

O Lady of Conquering Love, do conquer our hearts with your Immaculate loveliness, so that drawn from sinful ways to the precepts of your Son, we may glorify Him in this life, and, victoriously come to know Him, with you and all the Saints, forever in the next! Amen.

Bibliography

Beck, Warren. *New Mexico / A History of Four Centuries*. Norman: University of Oklahoma Press, 1977, seventh printing.

Chavez, Fráy Angélico. *La Conquistadora / The Autobiography of an Ancient Statue*. New Mexico: Sunstone Press. Revised Edition, 1975.

Chavez, Fráy Angélico. *My Penitente Land*. New Mexico: University of New Mexico Press, 1975.

Chavez, Fráy Angélico. *Our Lady of the Conquest*. New Mexico: Sunstone Press. New Edition, 2010.

Cook, Mary J. Straw. *Doña Tules / Santa Fe's Courtesan and Gambler*. Albuquerque:University of New Mexico Press, 2007.

Grimes, Ronald L. *Symbol and Conquest / Public Ritual and Drama in Santa Fe*. Albuquerque: University of New Mexico Press, 1992; Cornell University, 1976.

McCracken, Ellen, ed. *Fray Angélico Chávez /Poet, Priest, and Artist*. Albuquerque: University of New Mexico Press, 2000.

Noble, David Grant, editor. *Santa Fe / History of an Ancient City*. Santa Fe: School for Advanced Research Press, 2008.

Ribera-Ortega, Pedro. *La Conquistadora: America's Oldest Madonna*. New Mexico: Sunstone Press, 1975.

Ribera-Ortega, Pedro. *More Information on the Image and History of La Conquistadora* (Unpublished: Private collection), 2000.

Notes

1. Beck, Warren A., *New Mexico/A History of Four Centuries*. (University of Oklahoma Press, 1977), 84.

2. Luis Leal, "La Conquistadora as History & Fictitious Autobiography," *Fray Angélico Chávez/Poet, Priest, and Artist*. (Albuquerque: University of New Mexico Press, 2000), 41.

3. Luis Leal, "La Conquistadora as History & Fictitious Autobiography," *Fray Angélico Chávez/Poet, Priest, and Artist*. (Albuquerque: University of New Mexico Press, 2000), 43.

4. Chávez, Fray Angélico, *Our Lady of the Conquest*. (Santa Fe: Sunstone Press, 2010), 63.

5. Grimes, Ronald L. *Symbol and Conquest / Public Ritual and Drama in Santa Fe* (University of New Mexico Press, 1993), 191.

LaVergne, TN USA
15 October 2010
200754LV00002B/2/P